Second Edition

WRITE to be READ

Reading, Reflection, and Writing

WILLIAM R. SMALZER

CAMBRIDGE
UNIVERSITY PRESS

CAMBRIDGE UNIVERSITY PRESS
Cambridge, New York, Melbourne, Madrid, Cape Town, Singapore, São Paulo

Cambridge University Press
40 West 20th Street, New York, NY 10011-4211, USA

www.cambridge.org
Information on this title: www.cambridge.org/9780521547468

© Cambridge University Press 2005

This book is in copyright. Subject to statutory exception
and to the provisions of relevant collective licensing agreements,
no reproduction of any part may take place without
the written permission of Cambridge University Press.

First published 2005
2nd printing 2005

Printed in the United States of America

A catalog record for this publication is available from the British Library

Library of Congress Cataloging-in-Publication Data
Smalzer, William R.
   Write to read : reading, reflections, and writing / William R. Smalzer.—2nd ed.
   p. cm.
   ISBN 0-521-54746-6
   1. English language—Textbooks for foreign speakers. 2. English language—Rhetoric—Problems, exercises, etc. 3. Report writing—Problems, exercises, etc. 4. College readers. I. Title.

PE1128.S5816 2005
808'.042—dc22

2004065783

ISBN-13   978-0-521-54746-8 paperback
ISBN-10   0-521-54746-6 paperback

Cambridge University Press has no responsibility for
the persistence or accuracy of URLs for external or
third-party Internet Web sites referred to in this book,
and does not guarantee that any content on such
Web sites is, or will remain, accurate or appropriate.

Art direction and book design: Adventure House, NYC
Layout services: NK Graphics

CONTENTS

Plan of the Book iv

Preface vii

Text and Art Credits xii

1 **Birth Order and Your Place in Life** 1

2 **Matters of the Heart** 27

3 **Friendship** 55

4 **Live to Work or Work to Live?** 85

5 **Out of Courtesy** 113

6 **Questions of Right and Wrong** 139

7 **Progress and Tradition** 165

Appendix A: More on Grammar and
           Punctuation 191

Appendix B: Complete Essay
           Assessment Checklist 215

PLAN OF THE BOOK

CHAPTER	READINGS ON THE TOPIC
1 Birth Order and Your Place in Life	"How Your Birth Order Influences Your Life Adjustment" by *Lucille K. Forer* "Born for Each Other" by *Pamela Withers*
2 Matters of the Heart	"As It Was in the Beginning" by *E. Pauline Johnson* "The Lion's Hair" *Ethiopian Folktale*
3 Friendship	"The Friendship Bond" by *Mary Brown Parlee* "Heart Speaks to Heart Across a Cultural Divide" by *Gail Saunders*
4 Live to Work or Work to Live?	"The Ant and the Grasshopper" by *W. Somerset Maugham* "Mommy Wars, Part II" *Redbook Magazine*
5 Out of Courtesy	"Courtesy: Key to a Happier World" by *Dr. Norman Vincent Peale* "Tell White Lies (Occasionally)" by *Donald W. McCullough*
6 Questions of Right and Wrong	"A Gas Station Burns in the Forest" by *David A. Shapiro* "The Trumpet of Conscience" by *Dr. Martin Luther King, Jr.*
7 Progress and Tradition	"Modern Society and the Quest for Human Happiness" by the *Dalai Lama* "Development, Democracy, and the Village Telephone" by *Sam Pitroda*

FOCUS ON WRITING SKILLS	FORMAL WRITING ASSIGNMENT
• Paraphrasing • Writing topic sentences • Phrases, clauses, and fragments	Students write a paragraph presenting a point of view on birth order, supported with examples and paraphrasing.
• Summarizing • Patterns of paragraph organization • Correcting run-on sentences	Students write a paragraph about love, using one of the patterns of organization presented.
• More on paraphrasing • The essay and logical assertions • Thesis statements • Subject-verb agreement	Students write an essay about friendship, incorporating ideas from group discussion.
• Summarizing a story • Introductions and conclusions • Adding coherence	Students write an essay about work, integrating information from an interview.
• Outlining • Summarizing an article • Sentence variety: simple, compound, and complex	Students write an essay about manners, either from a cultural perspective or in response to a famous quotation.
• Summarizing a passage • Persuasive essays • Consistency in tense, person, number, and tone	Students write a persuasive essay about moral responsibility.
• Summarizing main ideas • Avoiding logical fallacies • Grammatical parallelism	Students write an argument essay based on a debate about progress and quality of life.

PREFACE

Overview

Write to Be Read: Reading, Reflection, and Writing is a high intermediate to advanced writing text designed to teach English language learners to write convincing paragraphs and academic essays with greater fluency. The second edition includes seven new readings and one completely new chapter, "Questions of Right and Wrong." In addition, more attention is given to reading preparation and vocabulary development. For the first of the two readings in each chapter, there is a vocabulary exercise which presents challenging vocabulary and also serves as a preview of the reading. For the second reading, which is generally shorter, important vocabulary is introduced in background notes and in the reflection and discussion activity.

Influenced by the whole language approach, **Write to Be Read** focuses primarily on discovering and communicating meaning rather than on learning discrete skills. The methodology is a blend of both the process and product approaches to writing. The process approach encourages students to develop their thinking about a topic through reading, writing, discussion, and revision. The product approach, relying heavily on student essays as models, helps writing students meet the expectations of their audience, educated readers of English.

Though much of writing is a solitary activity, **Write to Be Read** makes ample use of collaborative activities in discussions of readings and topics, in prewriting activities, and in peer review. The educational design of the book encourages students to think more clearly and critically and to develop their own voices as writers. The text also stresses the importance of summarizing and paraphrasing when using others' writing.

Readings include selections from nonfiction books, short stories, fables, essays, speeches, and magazine articles. Writing instruction concentrates on the academic essay, which is seen as the basis for other forms of academic writing. Of the seven chapters, the first two are devoted to paragraphs and the next five to essays. Chapters 6 and 7 discuss persuasive and argument essays. Appendix A has additional exercises on sentence structure, grammar, and punctuation for students who need such work. Appendix B gives complete essay assessment guidelines.

After becoming familiar with the topic of each chapter through reflection, discussion, and reading, students prepare for the formal writing assignment in stages. In each chapter, they begin with expressive writing and progress to more objective academic writing. First, in private journals, students respond subjectively to the main reading. Then they write responses that are more objective and share them with an audience of peers in Part 2. In Part 3, students read a second selection and think critically about the topic. After turning their attention to writing skills in Part 4, students begin the formal writing assignment in Part 5. They prepare a first draft after completing exercises designed to generate ideas and expand their points of view. Then they revise their first drafts, get feedback from peers, and revise further before submitting their essays for the teacher's evaluation.

Progressing from private, subjective writing to public, objective writing in each chapter helps students develop their thinking about topics one step at a time. It also develops a sense of audience and purpose in writing. The thinking/writing process is enhanced by collaborative work in which comprehension of meaning (the reader's goal) and expression of meaning (the writer's goal) guide most tasks.

Chapter Organization

1 INTRODUCTION TO THE TOPIC, READING, AND DISCUSSION

The first part of every chapter includes activities designed to develop schema and prepare students for the first reading selection. Through reflection on the topic, discussion, a vocabulary exercise, and notes on the first reading, students prepare to read. Comprehension questions lead students to read for the overall meaning first and then to delve more deeply as well as bring their own experience to the text.

2 PERSONAL WRITTEN RESPONSE

Students develop a sense of audience and voice by writing first for themselves and then for their classmates. In *Journals: A Private Audience,* they use journals to record their personal reactions to the main reading. Then, in *Shared Writing,* students write on topics that are more objective in nature and which require them to consider issues of logic and support. This writing is shared and discussed in small groups. To focus attention on content and ideas rather than on mechanics and spelling, students read their shared writings aloud.

3 FURTHER READING, WRITING, AND DISCUSSION

Part 3 contains the second reading selection on the chapter topic, which is from a different genre and features a different perspective. The second reading is usually shorter than the first, and students are helped with difficult vocabulary through background and language notes. Students negotiate the meaning of this second reading more independently, through writing a response to questions and sharing their writing in small groups. Part 3 ends with discussion questions designed to promote critical-thinking skills such as comparison, analysis, inference, and evaluation.

4 FOCUS ON WRITING SKILLS

Using Another's Writing, the first section in Part 4, contains either a summary or a paraphrase exercise intended to help students learn to incorporate others' ideas without plagiarizing them. Besides being a challenging language exercise, it serves as a review of one of the reading selections in the chapter. Students study matters of form, organization, and logic in *Meeting Reader Expectations.* They review common problems of sentence structure in the third section, *Sentence Grammar.*

5 FORMAL WRITING ASSIGNMENT

Parts 1–4 familiarize the students with the content and skills needed to write a formal, objective piece in this final part. Because **Write to Be Read** aims to help students improve their writing by developing their thinking, the first two sections in Part 5, *Generating Ideas* and *Expanding Your Point of View,* are important preliminaries to the formal writing assignment. In the *Initial Drafts* section, students are given guidelines as well as a checklist for first drafts and early revisions. *Review, Revision, and Assessment* guides students through further revision of their work. In this section, teachers review students' papers and may evaluate them or allow further revision, ideally at a later date, before assigning a grade.

Suggestions for Teaching and Assessment

Detailed suggestions for teaching each of the five parts are provided in the **Teacher's Manual**. In addition, the manual has specific notes for teaching each chapter. Listed below are some general teaching suggestions.

1 *Assign readings and drafts as homework.* To keep class lively, the readings in Parts 1 and 3 should be done by students at home and discussed in class. Likewise, initial drafts of paragraphs and essays can be written at home. However, students will benefit from occasionally writing in journals and doing the shared writing in Part 2 under time pressure in class because such exercises approximate exam situations.

2 *Use the photographs and illustrations to introduce topics.* Use the visuals at the beginning of Parts 1 and 3 as a warm-up, as a way to get students thinking about the topic, and as a means to elicit vocabulary related to the topic.

3 *Promote cooperation and collaboration.* Promote cooperation and collaboration among students by keeping the same small groups for *Feedback on Your Writing* (in Part 2), *Helping Each Other Understand* (in Part 3), *Expanding Your Point of View* (in Part 5), and *Peer Feedback* (also in Part 5) within the same chapter.

4 *Let students do their own writing.* Resist the temptation to take ownership of students' writing. Lead students to think, but do not think for them. If you wish, write the same assignments that your students do. Use your writing to illustrate revision, assessment, or other points. Sharing your writing with students takes courage but makes a valuable point: Even "good" writers need to revise.

5 *Have conferences with students.* Though schedules may not always allow, try to have a writing conference with each student, even for just two or three minutes, at some point during the drafting of each formal writing assignment. Students can learn to lead the conference by being ready to explain what stage they have reached in the writing process and what problems they are facing. The time is better spent if students ask you questions rather than vice versa. In a quick conference, it is better not to read a student's draft; there isn't enough time for you to judge the work fairly.

6 *Focus on writing, not grammar.* Help students realize that the course focuses more on clear writing than on correct grammar. Grammar does need to be dealt with, but it will keep the focus clearer if you refrain from marking every error. Instead, individualize grammar work by identifying for each student a few kinds of errors that occur in his or her work and assigning tasks that focus on these errors. Teaching grammar outside the context of the students' compositions keeps the course focus on thinking and writing about ideas. Your specific and positive written comments on content, word choice, organization, and other points will assure students that you have read their papers carefully. Positive comments are also more motivating than lots of grammar corrections.

7 *Revise in class.* Help students understand the revision process by revising together in class. Use a former student's paper or your own.

8 *Limit the number of revisions.* Given the choice between reworking the same paper over and over and going on to a new topic, teachers and students will find it more productive to go on to a new topic. Students will benefit more from reading, thinking, and writing about a new topic than from spending too much time revising an old paper. Revision of writing is important, of course; consider using the portfolio approach to evaluation so that several weeks elapse before a final revision on a paper is due.

9 *Distinguish between assessment and grades.* Make a distinction between assessment, which points out strengths and weaknesses, and evaluation, which involves assigning a holistic letter grade. Once a letter grade is put on a paper, students will give the essay little further serious thought or work.

10 *Use analytical assessment.* Use analytical assessment, based on the guidelines provided, so that students understand what is expected and how a weak paper can be improved. A *Paragraph Assessment Checklist* is provided at the ends of Chapters 1 and 2, and an *Essay Assessment Checklist* is provided at the ends of Chapters 3–7. Elements in the checklist vary according to the focus of each chapter.

Appendix B includes comprehensive essay assessment guidelines with the characteristics of very good, average, and weak essays in all three areas of assessment: (1) content and ideas, (2) organization and form, and (3) language use. Revise or replace the guidelines if they do not fit your way of teaching or your students.

11 *Model how to assess a paper.* As a class, assess an outside paper or one of the student models in the book so that students will know how to use the guidelines when they revise their own essays. Alternatively, give your students examples of what you consider very good, average, and weak essays. Use papers from a previous class to avoid embarrassment.

12 *Give three separate scores.* When assessing a paper, give three separate scores, one each for content and ideas, organization and form, and language use so that students understand their strengths and weaknesses. For example, an analytical assessment of 8/10 (8 out of a possible score of 10) for content and ideas,

4/5 for organization and form, and 1/5 for language use indicates that the student has done well in two out of three areas. Weighting content and ideas twice as heavily as the other two categories lets students know that you feel that the logic, clarity, and sincerity of the thoughts expressed are the most important aspects of their papers.

13 *Use a portfolio approach.* If it works for your class, use a portfolio approach for evaluation. Rather than evaluate the formal writing assignments with a letter grade, assess them using the assessment guidelines and numerical scores. Then allow students to revise one of their previously assessed papers for a midterm grade and another paper for a final grade. The portfolio approach allows students to come back to their writing later with more insights into the topic, perhaps, and with a better idea of rhetorical and language conventions because of intervening study. To avoid inflated grades, some teachers average the scores on successive revisions rather than considering only the last, best effort.

William R. Smalzer

TEXT CREDITS

Page 6: From *Birth Order and Life Roles* by Lucille K. Forer, 1969. Courtesy of Charles C. Thomas Publisher, Ltd., Springfield, Illinois.

Page 14: "Born for Each Other?" by Pamela Withers, *McCall's Magazine*, February 1989. Reprinted by permission of the author.

Pages 29, 32: From "As It Was in the Beginning" by E. Pauline Johnson, from *Moccasin Maker*, University of Arizona Press, 1987.

Page 38: "The Lion's Hair" by William J. Bennett. Reprinted with the permission of Simon & Schuster Adult Publishing Group from *The Moral Compass* by William J. Bennett. Copyright © 1995 William J. Bennett.

Page 59: "The Friendship Bond" by Mary Brown Parlee. Reprinted with permission from *Psychology Today Magazine.* Copyright © 1979, Sussex Publishers, Inc.

Page 65: "Heart Speaks to Heart Across a Cultural Divide" by Gail Saunders. *The Christian Science Monitor,* Aug. 2, 2000. Reprinted by permission of the author.

Page 86: "The Ant and the Grasshopper," from *Aesop & Company.* Text copyright © 1991 by Barbara Bader. Reprinted by permission of Houghton Mifflin Company. All rights reserved.

Page 90: Excerpted from "The Ant and the Grasshopper" by W. Somerset Maugham from *The Complete Stories of W. Somerset Maugham* published by William Heinemann. Used by permission of The Random House Group Limited. U.S. rights with permission from Trustees of the William Somerset Maugham Estate, Macondo Arts, London.

Page 96: "The Mommy Wars, Part II," *Redbook Magazine,* June 2000. Reprinted with permission of Hearst Communications, Inc.

Page 117: From "Courtesy: Key to a Happier World" by Dr. Norman Vincent Peale. *Saturday Evening Post,* May/June 1975. Reprinted with permission from the Ruth S. Peale Marital Trust.

Page 123: "Tell White Lies (Occasionally)" from *Say Please, Say Thank You* by Donald W. McCullough, copyright © 1998 by Donald W. McCullough. Used by permission of G.P. Putnam's Sons, a division of Penguin Group (USA) Inc.

Page 143: "A Gas Station Burns in the Forest: Illuminating Our Moral Legacy," from *Choosing the Right Thing to Do,* 1999, by David A. Shapiro, Berrett-Koehler Publishers, Inc., San Francisco, CA. Reprinted with permission of the publisher. All rights reserved. www.bkconnection.com.

Pages 150, 152: "The Trumpet of Conscience" by Dr. Martin Luther King Jr. Reprinted by arrangement with the Estate of Martin Luther King Jr., c/o Writers

House as agent for the proprietor, New York, NY. Copyright © 1967 by Martin Luther King Jr., copyright renewed 1991 Coretta Scott King.

Page 169: "Modern Society and the Quest for Human Happiness," from *Ethics for the New Millennium* by Dalai Lama and Alexander Norman, copyright ©1999 by His Holiness The Dalai Lama. Used by permission of Riverhead Books, an imprint of Penguin Group (USA) Inc. Used by permission of the Wylie Agency Inc., New York, NY.

Page 176: From "Development, Democracy, and the Village Telephone" by Sam (Satyan) Pitroda, *Harvard Business Review* Nov/Dec 1993. Reprinted by permission of *Harvard Business Review*. Copyright © 1993 by the Harvard Business School Publishing Corporation. All rights reserved.

Pages 71, 102, 127, and 181: The essays on these pages were contributed by students whose names appear following their work.

ART CREDITS

Illustration Credits: pages 37, 64, 113, 121, and 139: Paul Antonson; page 85: Randy Jones

Photo Credits: page 1: ©Taxi/Getty Images; page 12: ©Taxi/Getty Images, © Thinkstock, ©Ondrea Barbe/Corbis; page 27: ©Superstock, ©Getty Images; page 55: ©Richard Hutchings/PhotoEdit, ©Getty Images, ©A.G.E. Fotostock; page 95: ©Javier Larrea/Age Fotostock, ©A. Ramey/Woodfin Camp, ©NDX Photos/Newscom; page 149: ©AP/Wide World Photo; page 165; ©Bob Daemmrich/The Image Works, ©Signar-ITAR-TASS/Newscom; page 174: ©Tom Tracy Photography/Alamy

CHAPTER 1

Birth Order and Your Place in Life

- Do children raised in the same family end up with similar personalities? Why or why not?
- What shapes a child's personality?

PART 1

INTRODUCTION TO THE TOPIC, READING, AND DISCUSSION

A Reflection

Make a list of the children in your family, from oldest to youngest, and include your name in the list. Write each name on a different line. Then look at the adjectives and phrases in the box. Write these words next to the names they describe. (A word may apply to more than one person, but assign it to the person who comes to mind first.)

_____

_____

_____

_____

_____

_____

capable
confident
fast learner
flexible
independent
parental
protected by parents
responsible
sometimes lonely
tattletale*
unusually dependent on parents

tattletale: *one who "tattles," or reports, to adults when someone else misbehaves*

Follow-up Compare your list with a classmate's. Are there any similarities in the descriptions you chose for the oldest child? The youngest?

B Discussion

Read each statement, and write *A* if you agree with it and *D* if you disagree. Then discuss your answers in pairs or small groups.

_____ 1 Older children in a family are often parental and bossy toward the younger children.

_____ 2 Parents are more relaxed and less excited about their second- and third-born children.

_____ 3 Older children are more responsible because the younger siblings depend on them.

_____ 4 Youngest children are often spoiled* because of all the care and attention they receive. They may pout* when they don't get their own way.

_____ 5 In smaller families there is little competition among the children for their parents' love and attention.

_____ 6 When there is a fight between an older and a younger sibling, parents will usually take the side of the younger one and protect him or her.

_____ 7 Parents are less strict* with their first children than with their later ones.

_____ 8 Most children who are difficult and demand a lot of attention will grow up to be difficult people.

pout: *act or look bad-tempered and silent*
spoiled: *harmed by too little discipline and too much attention*
strict: *setting many rules that must be obeyed*

C Preparing to read

NOTES ON THE READING

It is interesting to notice that in a family with several children, the children are usually very different from each other. To explain the differences, some psychologists point out that even with the same parents, each child's environment is a little different. Furthermore, each child reacts to his or her environment differently because of differences in personality.

In "How Your Birth Order Influences Your Life Adjustment," Lucille K. Forer explains the differences between siblings by looking at their birth order. According to this reading, whether one is an only child, the oldest, a middle, or the youngest child determines to a great extent the kind of person that one will become.

This chapter from a book is written in an academic style, and uses many long sentences. You will find it easier to read by breaking up very long sentences into meaningful parts like this:

The first and most obvious effect / of taking a certain position in the family / is the relationship we have / with respect to the people / already there.

PREVIEWING THE VOCABULARY

Before reading, preview the vocabulary in context. Read these key sentences based on the selection and choose the best meaning for the underlined words.

1 When we are born into a family unit or brought into it through adoption or as a step-child, we take a certain place in the family hierarchy.

   a. history

   b. house or apartment

   c. system of power and authority

Birth Order and Your Place in Life

2. The first child <u>imitates</u> the parents' physical mannerisms and learns speech from them.
   a. learns
   b. copies
   c. looks at

3. A first child learns many things, and much of the learning is on an unconscious level. That is, neither the parents nor the child <u>verbalizes</u> that thus and so is the way to do something.
   a. say
   b. argue
   c. show, demonstrate

4. If there are only adults present with a child, the adults are in a very close, intense relationship with the child, as anyone who has watched first-time parents <u>hovering over</u> their infants knows.
   a. leaving unattended
   b. keeping others away from
   c. standing nearby and watching closely

5. The only child never has any reason to change this <u>perception</u> of his role, and he tends to carry into adulthood a strong feeling of being a child in relation to other people.
   a. love
   b. strength
   c. understanding

6. When a sibling arrives, the first child tries to <u>suppress</u> the view of himself as a child and he struggles to be parental.
   a. continue
   b. exaggerate
   c. stop; keep hidden or secret

7. Later children <u>benefit</u> from the tendency of parents to try out ideas on their first child and to be more tolerant with later children.
   a. suffer
   b. receive an advantage
   c. understand their place in the family

8. After testing <u>judgments</u> about matters ranging from when to toilet train a first child to attitudes about dating, parents are more relaxed with later children.
   a. results
   b. students
   c. decisions

9 The first child serves as a <u>barrier</u> between later children and the parents. Later children see less of their parents than the first child did.
   a. messenger
   b. wall; obstacle
   c. line of communication

10 Later children do not feel the same dependency on the parents for <u>sustenance</u> and companionship as did the first child.
   a. company
   b. food and care
   c. rules; discipline

11 Because they have an older sibling to turn to, later children do not feel as lonely or as inadequate when they do not <u>meet the standards</u> of their parents.
   a. follow the rules
   b. become exact copies
   c. reach the expectations

12 Since later children do not have as much direct <u>identification with their parents</u>, the children do not try as hard to be adult during childhood.
   a. dislike of their parents
   b. feeling of being like their parents
   c. feeling of being different from their parents

13 Older children tend to develop a <u>self-concept</u> that includes the belief that "I can do many things better than my siblings can."
   a. loneliness
   b. self-confidence
   c. view of themselves

14 Since she feels she can do many things better, she feels <u>more adequate</u> than other people in many situations.
   a. busier
   b. more patient
   c. more capable

Follow-up Check and discuss your answers in pairs or with the class.

D Reading for overall meaning

Read the selection at a quick but comfortable pace. As you read, think about this question:

How accurate is the author's description of your birth order? Explain.

How Your Birth Order Influences Your Life Adjustment

Lucille K. Forer

When we are born into a family unit or brought into it through adoption or as a step-child, we take a certain place in the family hierarchy. We become *only* child, *oldest* child, *middle* child, or *youngest* child.

The first and most obvious effect of taking a certain position in the family is the relationship we have with respect to the people already there. If there are only adults present, we are in a very close and often intense relationship with them, as anyone knows who has had a child or who has watched first-time parents hovering over their infants. This constant and close relationship gives the first child in the family an opportunity to imitate and learn from these adults to the fullest possible extent. The first child imitates their physical mannerisms and learns speech from them. He learns many more things and much of the learning takes place on an unconscious level. That is, neither the parents nor the child verbalizes that thus and so is the way to do something. The child observes and imitates.

Relationship with Parents

From the beginning the parents treat the child in accordance with his place in the family, and soon the child recognizes that place. He is the child in the family, and he tends to think of himself as a child in relation to adults. The only child never has any reason to change this perception of his role and he tends to carry into adulthood a strong feeling of being a child in relation to other people.

The first child, who becomes the older or oldest child, does not have this unlimited time to view himself as the child in the relationship with his parents. When a sibling arrives, he tries to suppress the view of himself as a child, and he struggles to be parental. We shall find that in both childhood and adulthood, the older or oldest child's emphasis upon being "parental" offers him both advantages and problems.

Children who follow the first child in the family come into a situation where the relationship with the parent is, except in the most unusual cases, shared with another child. The parents themselves have been changed by the preceding child or children in many ways. They are more experienced as parents. They

continued

may not welcome their later children with as much delight as they did their first child, but they are probably less tense and anxious about being able to care for them properly. The later children enjoy many advantages as a result of having more relaxed parents. They benefit from the tendency of parents to try out ideas on their first child and to be more tolerant with later children. After testing judgments about matters ranging from when to toilet train a child to attitudes about dating, parents are relatively certain of approaches to take with later children, and they are usually more relaxed (and exhausted) ones.

The first child serves as a barrier between later children and the parents. He is one of the models for his siblings. Later children in a family do not feel the same dependency on the parents for sustenance and companionship that the first child did. They have a "peer" to turn to when the parents are not available. Consequently they do not have such intense feelings of loneliness when the attention of the parents is directed elsewhere, nor do they seem to feel so inadequate when they do not meet the standards of their parents.

Extremely important to differentiating later children from first children is the extent to which direct identification with the parents is diluted for the later children. The later children seem more content to move gradually from child to adult. They do not seem to try as hard, as does the oldest child, to be parental and adult even during childhood.

How Children See Themselves and Others

The child becomes known as the family's only child, oldest child, middle child, or youngest child, depending on his birth order. He is thought and talked about as having that place in the family. Both in his mind and in the minds of other people an important part of his identity is his family position.

The other members of the family assume certain attitudes toward each child in terms of his birth order. Parents usually expect their oldest child to be more capable and more responsible than the younger children. The oldest child comes to think about himself in the same way. These ways of seeing himself, of thinking about himself because of his sibling role, become part of his self-concept.

Older or oldest brother or sister tends to develop a self-concept that includes the belief that "I can do many things better than my siblings can. I am more adequate than other people in many situations."

The middle child comes to think of himself as sometimes better able to do things than other people because he is usually more capable than his younger sibling or siblings. Sometimes, though, he must turn to his older sibling or to his parents for help, and so he comes to think of himself as able to obtain help when he needs it.

The youngest child tends to think, "I am less able to do many things than other people. But I need not be concerned because there are always others around to take care of me."

continued

The role we take as the result of being in a certain place in the family not only causes us to think about ourselves in certain ways, it also causes us to think about other people in certain ways. The oldest tends to expect other people to be relatively less capable. The middle child has less specific expectations about the capabilities of other people. The youngest may see others as more adequate while the only child tends to think, "I am most secure when there are parents around to take care of me, but when they are not there, I have no one to turn to for help. So I'd better learn to take care of myself as much as possible."

The place in the family establishes for the child a specific role to be played within the family group. It influences him to develop certain attitudes toward himself and toward other people and helps him develop specific patterns of behavior.

Follow-up Now answer the question below:

How accurate is the author's description of your birth order? Explain.

Reading for more detail

Read the article a second time. This exercise will help you read for more detail and bring your experience to the reading.

1 As you read, take notes by filling in the grid with phrases that characterize each birth order.

Oldest child:
Later children (both middle and youngest):
Middle child:
Youngest child:
Only child:

2 Think of family members or friends for each of the birth orders. How well do the author's descriptions fit them?

3 Which birth order results in the most responsible child? The least responsible?

4 In what ways might an only child become more independent than a middle or youngest child?

5 *Key words* Make a list of six words or expressions that seem important to the article. Be ready to explain what each word means and why it is important. Here is an example.

> <u>unconscious</u>: without being aware, without knowing. This is an important word because it explains how children learn their birth-order behavior, without parents realizing they're actually teaching this to the child.

Follow-up Discuss your answers in pairs, in small groups, or as a class.

PART 2
PERSONAL WRITTEN RESPONSE

Ⓐ Journals: A private audience

Choose two of the following topics. Write for about 20 minutes in your journal notebook. Express your opinions and feelings honestly. These journal entries are for your eyes only, so do not spend a lot of time using a dictionary or worrying about grammar.

1 Did you like this reading? Why or why not?

2 Did the author's descriptions remind you of anyone you know? Who? In what ways?

3 Does this reading make sense to you? Do you find it believable and logical?

Ⓑ Shared writing

Choose two topics and write for a total of 20 minutes. Your audience is your classmates, with whom you will share your writing. They will be interested not only in *what* you feel but also in *why* you feel that way. Therefore, you will want to express your views clearly and support them.

1 Do you think the author's discussion applies more to the typical family in the United States (mother, father, and two children) than to families in general? Explain.

2 Is Forer's discussion of birth order accurate or inaccurate for the children in your family? Explain.

3 Can you think of another explanation for the differences between children in the same family? Explain.

Ⓒ Feedback on your writing

Get feedback on how clear and logical your thinking and writing are. Select one of the questions from *Shared Writing* and read your answer to a small group of classmates. Follow the guidelines on the next page for giving peer feedback.

Peer Feedback Guidelines

Writers

- Read your paper out loud to the group, and read it a second time if necessary.
- Respond to listeners' comments and questions.
- Ask for suggestions if you want them.

Listeners

- You may wish to take notes while listening to the writer read. Then briefly summarize what you have understood.
- Ask questions about parts that are not clear. If you wish, share with the group how the writing makes you feel.
- Do not make negative comments or tell the writer what changes to make.

PART 3
FURTHER READING, WRITING, AND DISCUSSION

One of these couples doesn't seem to be getting along well. Do you think that the birth order of each partner might play a role in the success of a relationship?

A Preparing to read

NOTES ON THE READING

"Born for Each Other?" has a lighter style than the previous reading. In this magazine article, the writer has two purposes: to inform and to entertain the reader. The topic—what makes two people a good match for each other—is of interest to most people. The title of the article borrows from an expression one often hears when people talk of a good match. If a man and a woman are "born for each other," they are perfect for each other in every way.

REFLECTION AND DISCUSSION

Look at the descriptions of different men and women. From your experience, which pairs do you think would make good matches? Draw a line between each good match. Find a match for all six people.

Men		Women	
1	He grew up with younger sisters, so he is very indulgent* towards women. He is charmed by them and will give his wife whatever she wants without expecting much from her. He can be a little headstrong,* though.	a	She can be very parental, probably because she took care of younger siblings growing up. She is confident, responsible, and reserved.* However, she tends to be domineering (i.e., she expects others to do what she wants).
2	He was the baby in his family. He needs a lot of attention but isn't very ambitious. He is good at manipulating* others to get what he wants. He succeeds by being charming—or if necessary, by pouting.	b	She grew up with several older brothers, so she is a tomboy, a girl who likes rough, noisy activities. Because she's playful, she likes to flirt* with men. She needs a man who will appreciate these qualities.
3	As an only child, he grew up being the apple of his father's eye.* Therefore, he is used to constant attention and approval. Thus, he's not very good at giving.	c	She had a lot of younger brothers, so she values men and is a good sport (i.e., an easygoing person who gets along in any situation and with anybody). She is a very nurturing* person.

apple of somebody's eye: *person that is loved more than any other*
flirt: *show romantic interest in someone without any serious intentions*
headstrong: *determined to do things in one's own way without listening to others*
indulgent: *allowing someone to have whatever she wants or likes*
manipulating: *controlling somebody cleverly but unfairly*
nurturing: *good at taking care of others*
reserved: *slow to show emotions or express opinions*

Follow-up Discuss your answers in pairs, in small groups, or as a class.

B Reading for overall meaning

Before you read, think of couples you know (and whose birth orders you know). Choose one couple that is happily married and another couple that is not happily married. Keep these marriages in mind as you read "Born for Each Other?" Read the selection the first time to answer this question:

Does the article explain why the two marriages you chose above are happy or unhappy marriages?

Born for Each Other?

Pamela Withers

Ronald and Lois, married for two decades, consider themselves a happy couple, but in the early years of their marriage, both were disturbed by persistent arguments that seemed to fade away without ever being truly resolved. They uncovered clues to what was going wrong by researching a fascinating subject: how birth order (whether you came along first, second or later in your family) affects not only your personality, but also how compatible you are with your mate!

Ronald and Lois are only children, and "onlies" grow up accustomed to being the apples of their parents' eyes. They're not necessarily spoiled—just used to constant attention and approval. Match two onlies and you have partners who subconsciously expect each other to continue fulfilling this expectation, while neither has much experience in the "giving" end. The habit of trying to dominate a relationship and taking it personally when your spouse does the same can result in quarrels that sound alike from one onlies household to another.

All those patterns set in motion by birth and gender order don't prescribe what must occur; they simply describe tendencies that may need to be recognized or overcome.

Here's a list of common birth-order characteristics—and some thoughts on the best (and worst) marital matches for each:

Oldest Child

The oldest tends to be self-assured, responsible, a high achiever, and relatively serious and reserved, with parental qualities as a result of caring for younger siblings. He may become a perfectionist and worrier who finds it difficult to take criticism or tolerate others' mistakes, and he may be slow to make friends, perhaps content with only one companion.

The more "same sex" siblings an oldest has, the more independent and domineering he or she is and the more difficult it may be for him or her to find a suitable mate. The best matches are with a youngest, an only, or a mate raised

continued

with a large number of opposite-sex siblings. The worst match is with another oldest of same-sex siblings, since the two will be too sovereign to share a household comfortably. The oldest sister of brothers is popular because she values men and is a good sport. She matches well with a youngest, whom she can lead and nurture. The oldest brother of sisters tends to be easygoing, fun-loving, considerate, and very fond of women. He is good at pleasing all females and is especially well matched with the youngest sister of brothers.

Youngest Child

The baby of the family thrives on attention and tends to be outgoing, adventurous, optimistic, creative, easygoing and less ambitious than others in the family. He may lack self-discipline and have difficulty making decisions on his own. The youngest may learn to manipulate, either by pouting or by being charming.

A younger sister of sisters will match best with an oldest sibling, who will see through her manipulation and is charmed by her playfulness. A youngest brother of brothers, often headstrong, unpredictable, and romantic, will match best with an oldest or middle sister of brothers, whom he will allow to control his life in an unobtrusive manner. The youngest of same-sex siblings should avoid each other, since neither is nurturing, nor are they accustomed to members of the opposite sex. The youngest sister of brothers, often a tomboy and a flirt, is best matched with an oldest brother of sisters, who will happily indulge these traits. She's smart to stay away from an oldest brother of brothers or, worse, a youngest brother of brothers. The youngest brother of sisters is popular because he enjoys women who are supportive, admiring, and eager to please.

Middle Child

The middle child is influenced by many variables; however, middles are often introverted, less likely to take initiative or achieve high academic standards, and more anxious and self-critical than others.

The middle child's most comfortable marriage duplicates a relationship with a close sibling. Middles often successfully marry other middles, since both are strong on tact, not so strong on aggressiveness and tend to crave affection.

Only Child

The only child picks up characteristics of her same-sex parent's birth order, and this may influence who represents her best match. She is often most comfortable when alone, but since an "only" tends to be a well-adjusted individual, she'll eventually learn to relate to any chosen spouse.

continued

> The male only child expects his wife to make life easier without getting much in return; he is sometimes best matched with a younger or middle sister of brothers, or a maternal, oldest sister of brothers. His most difficult match is with another only. The female only child, who tends to be slightly more flexible, is well matched with an older man, who will indulge her tendency to test his love. Any birth order will do, but her best match is apt to be a brother of sisters. Her worst match? Another only, of course.

Follow-up Now answer this question:

Does the article explain why the two marriages you chose on page 14 are happy or unhappy marriages?

C Reading for more detail

Read the selection again. Mark any places in the text that are still unclear to you.

D Helping each other understand

Write for about 20 minutes on one or more of the questions below.

1 What do you have trouble understanding in the selection?

2 Does the article seem logical to you? Explain.

3 Are the personality descriptions accurate for the couples you chose in *Reading for Overall Meaning* on page 14.

Follow-up To a small group of students, read what you have written. Read your reaction a second time if necessary. Each group member will respond with (1) a question, (2) a comment, and/or (3) help with what you didn't understand.

E Discussion: Critical thinking

Discuss these questions in pairs, in small groups, or as a class.

1 The audiences for the two readings in this chapter are different. Forer's audience might be a university psychology class, and Withers' audience might be the general public. The writers therefore chose different subject matter and wrote in different styles. How are the subject matter and style different in the two readings?

2 Withers tells us that the birth order of spouses can affect the success of their marriage. Do you think people's birth order also affects their choices of friends? Who they choose to work with? Explain.

3 Some psychologists criticize birth-order theory as wrong and unscientific. What is your position? Do you find the birth-order theory believable? Explain.

PART 4
FOCUS ON WRITING SKILLS

A Using another's writing: Paraphrasing

For your formal writing assignment in this chapter, you will write one or more paragraphs on birth order and/or children in a family. If you use Forer's or Withers' ideas on birth order in your writing, you will need to *paraphrase* their ideas, which means to express them in your own words. There are two reasons to paraphrase. First, you want your audience to know that you understand the ideas and are not just copying them from the text. Second, using someone else's words as your own is *plagiarism*. Plagiarism is considered dishonest in academic circles and many cultures. Plagiarism makes it impossible to know the original source of the information or ideas.

EXERCISE 1 *Paraphrasing sentences*

Paraphrase the Forer quotations that follow. First, find the sentence in the text (page 6–8) and carefully read it in context (the lines before and after). Then rewrite the sentence in your own words, changing the structure of the original sentence. Do not use the words in italics. A suggested beginning is given to help you. Finally, revise your sentence to make your paraphrase clear and accurate.

1 (lines 16–17) ". . . the parents *treat* the child *in accordance with his place* in the family, and soon the child recognizes that place."

> Paraphrase: The child in a family learns his place in the family from the way that his parents behave with him, which is determined by that child's birth order.
>
> Revision: The child learns his role in the family from his parents' behavior with him, which is influenced by the child's birth order.

2 (lines 23–24) "When a sibling arrives, he tries to *suppress the view* of himself as a child, and he *struggles* to be parental."

The oldest child . . .

3 (lines 35–36) "[Later children] *benefit* from the *tendency* of parents to *try out ideas* on their first child and to be more tolerant with later children."

Later children are better off because . . .

4 (lines 47–49) "Extremely important to *differentiating* later children from first children is the extent to which direct *identification* with the parents is *diluted* for the later children."

One very important way that later children differ . . .

5 (lines 55–56) "Both *in his mind* and *in the minds* of other people, an important part of his *identity* is his family position."

The child's position in the family determines . . .

B Meeting reader expectations: Writing topic sentences

Simply put, a paragraph is an indented block of writing that expresses one main idea. While not all writers actually state the main idea in every paragraph, it is useful for students trying to improve their writing to express the main idea in a *topic sentence.* Beginning a paragraph with a topic sentence helps you decide which details would support your main idea. By letting the topic sentence guide your choice of supporting details, you will write a unified paragraph, a paragraph that sticks to its main idea without losing the point.

EXERCISE 2 *The main idea*

Read this model paragraph and answer the questions that follow.

> There are obviously factors other than birth order that affect how we deal with other people. Our society plays a big role. Some societies are very communal, so people other than parents are very involved in raising the children. Heredity is also important in differentiating siblings from each other. Many experts accept that characteristics like temperament, sensitivity to the environment, and intelligence are inherited. These characteristics vary from child to child in the same family; they also play a role in the child's personality. In addition, our parents themselves are a big factor in determining what kind of people we are. From them we learn to be cheerful, kind, helpful people—or not. The issue of how we are as people is a complicated one; birth order plays a role, but so do factors like society, heredity, and parents.

1 Is the main idea expressed in a topic sentence by the author? If so, underline it.

2 How many points of support are there for the main idea? Number them. Briefly, what are the main points of support?

3 Is the paragraph *complete,* that is, are there enough details to convince you of the author's main idea?

4 Is this paragraph unified? Does it stick to the main idea without losing the point? Explain.

5 What is the function of the last sentence in the paragraph?

EXERCISE 3 *Topic sentences*

A good topic sentence satisfies the following two criteria:
- The topic is *narrow* enough to cover in a paragraph.
- The statement about the topic is *specific,* but general enough to lead to a well-developed paragraph.

Look at these topic sentences with a partner. Discuss whether they meet the two criteria.

1. Psychology is an interesting subject to study.
2. I wanted to sign up for the adolescent psychology course, but the class was already full.
3. When a boy in my country turns eight, he faces a number of new responsibilities.
4. B. F. Skinner was a famous American psychologist who studied the learning process.
5. Children who grow up without siblings usually learn to play well by themselves.
6. Children in my country are more dependent than children in the United States.
7. Research has shown that children from happy marriages are more likely to have successful marriages themselves.
8. Children are always interesting to watch.

Sentence grammar: Phrases, clauses, and fragments

PHRASES AND CLAUSES

A *phrase* is a group of related words that may include either a subject or a verb, but does not include both. A phrase cannot stand alone because it is not a sentence; it is only part of a sentence. The example below shows several different kinds of phrases.

Birth-order theory	has been used	to explain differences	in siblings.
noun phrase	**verb phrase**	**infinitive phrase**	**prepositional phrase**

Prepositional phrases are sometimes troublesome for students because these phrases can make it difficult to identify the subject and verb in a sentence. Prepositional phrases begin with prepositions (e.g., *from, in, with, by*). They also contain a noun (e.g., *beginning, place, family*) or a gerund (e.g., *pouting, being*) as an object of the preposition.

Look at the following sentences. Each prepositional phrase is underlined, and each preposition is in italics.

  a. *From* the beginning the parents treat the child *in* accordance *with* his place *in* the family.
  b. The youngest may learn to manipulate, either *by* pouting or being charming.

Recognizing prepositional phrases in a sentence will help you understand the structure of a sentence.

A *clause* is a group of related words that contains both a subject and a complete verb that has tense (e.g., *went, is going, has gone,* and so on). Clauses can be *independent* or *dependent.*

An *independent clause* expresses a complete thought, so it can stand alone as a sentence. Examples *a* and *b* are independent clauses. The subjects are underlined, and the verbs are in italics.

a. Not everyone *agrees* about the effects of birth order.

b. But birth order *helps* to explain some differences in siblings.

A *dependent clause* is not a sentence because it doesn't express a complete thought. It cannot stand alone; it must appear with an independent clause. A dependent clause begins with a subordinating conjunction (a word like *because, when, while, although, if, whereas,* or *since*) or a relative pronoun (e.g., *who, which, that,* and so on). Examples *c* and *d* are dependent clauses.

c. . . . because there *are* many influences on personality . . .

d. . . . who *are born* later . . .

EXERCISE 4 *Adding phrases and dependent clauses to independent clauses*

Read each independent clause below. Add one or both of the phrases/dependent clauses in parentheses to make a more complete and more logical sentence. You can add to the beginning or end of the independent clause. Do not add a phrase or clause if it is not logical. Then write your new sentence.

1. The Egyptian family is often an extended family.
   (. . . , which includes other relatives / . . . with no adults other than the parents living there)

   The Egyptian family is often an extended family, which includes other relatives.

2. In Egypt relatives are more likely to live with a family.
   (. . . who don't really like the family / . . . than they are in many western countries)

3. There may be more resources for the children.
   (. . . like attention and affection / with other adult relatives in the household . . .)

4. This extended family configuration probably changes the effects.
   (because it results in smaller families, . . . / . . . of birth order)

5 There may be less competition among siblings.
   (. . . for the parents' affection / when then are fewer adults in the house, . . .)
   _____
   _____

6 It would be surprising, however.
   (. . . if none of the ideas about birth order were correct for Egypt / . . . to most of us)
   _____
   _____

7 We would still expect the oldest child to be more responsible.
   (for example, . . . / . . . in comparison with his brothers and sisters)
   _____
   _____

FRAGMENTS

In formal writing every sentence must be grammatical. A grammatical sentence must have at least one independent clause with a subject and a complete verb that has tense. The independent clause must express a complete thought.

Sometimes what looks like a sentence is not a sentence. Look at these examples:

   a. Finishing my homework before going to bed.
   b. Because I got up late this morning.

These examples are not sentences. Example *a* is a phrase with no complete verb or subject. Example *b* is a dependent clause. It is an incomplete thought that can't stand alone. Although the examples are written as complete sentences with capital letters and periods, these examples are *fragments* because they are not independent clauses.

EXERCISE 5 *Identifying fragments*

Read each item and underline any fragments. If there is no fragment, write *OK*. For each fragment, write the letter of the reason (*a* or *b*) in the blank.

   a. It is a dependent clause.
   b. It is a phrase that lacks a complete verb and/or a subject.

   _____ 1 Parents try to give a fair share of the family's resources to each child. In order to distribute the resources evenly.

   _____ 2 The children themselves are not so interested in an even distribution of resources. They compete. Because each one wants as much as possible of the parents' time and attention.

   _____ 3 Smaller children usually learn that they can compete with older ones. Despite their small size.

_____ 4 Because they are smaller and weaker, younger children can usually count on the help of the parents in a dispute with siblings. Most parents will get involved.

_____ 5 Younger children learn to use their smallness and weakness to their advantage. They can easily become tattletales. Or even crybabies.

_____ 6 A tattletale reports misdeeds of a sibling to parents. For example, the tattletale will say things like, "Mommy, Bobbie hit me again!"

_____ 7 A crybaby soon learns the power of tears to get what he or she wants. And to win in a conflict with an older sibling.

CORRECTING FRAGMENTS ··

You can correct a fragment by (1) connecting it to an independent clause, or (2) adding the necessary words to make it into an independent clause. Look at these examples:

FRAGMENT   In a dispute between siblings, parents usually take the side of the younger child. Because that child is weaker and smaller.

CORRECTION TYPE 1   In a dispute between siblings, parents usually take the side of the younger child because that child is weaker and smaller.

CORRECTION TYPE 2   In a dispute between siblings, parents usually take the side of the younger child. They do so because that child is weaker and smaller.

EXERCISE 6 *Correcting fragments*

Read each item and underline any fragments. Then rewrite the entire item, correcting the fragments using correction type 1 or type 2.

1 Two only children who marry each other may have problems. Because both are used to a lot of attention and approval.

2 An oldest child may find that another oldest is not a good marriage match. An oldest may be happier with an only child. Or with a youngest child.

3 A youngest sister of sisters matches best with an oldest brother. Who will appreciate her charm. Also tolerate her manipulation.

4 The best match for a middle child is often another middle child. Since both are tactful. And normally not aggressive.

5 Although only children find it easier to make good matches. There are bad matches for them. Such as another only.

EXERCISE 7 *Editing for fragments*

Read the paragraph that follows. Then reread the paragraph and follow these steps:

1 Underline all fragments.
2 Rewrite the whole paragraph, correcting the fragments by connecting them to other sentences or by adding the necessary words to make them independent clauses.

   Critics of birth-order theory say that it is not scientific. Because one cannot prove it. And because it is like astrology. Interesting, perhaps, but not to be taken seriously. Supporters of birth-order theory admit that it alone does not determine what kind of people we are. Our parents and society, for example, are strong influences. Whether we are happy or gloomy, calm or nervous, or good-natured or bad-tempered people. However, birth order does play a role. Determining the degree to which a child is happy, calm, and good-natured, for example. It plays another role. In determining how a child uses his or her happiness, calmness, and good-naturedness in dealing with other people.

PART 5

FORMAL WRITING ASSIGNMENT

Ⓐ Writing topics

Choose a writing topic from the list below. For your formal writing assignment, you will develop a paragraph on the topic you choose.

1. Paraphrase what Forer and/or Withers say about your birth order. Then compare what they say with how you actually see yourself. How closely do the authors' ideas match your view of yourself? Write a topic sentence that lets readers know how closely your views match those of the authors.

2. People with which birth order seem to have the easiest lives? The most difficult ones? The happiest ones? The most appealing lives? Choose one and describe it by telling what makes those lives easy, difficult, happy, or attractive.

3. Choose a couple you know well. How successful is their relationship? Use birth-order theory to explain and support your observations about their relationship.

4. Relate a true incident that illustrates a point about birth order. Make that point clear in your topic sentence.

Ⓑ Generating ideas: Free writing

1. Write freely for 15 or 20 minutes on your topic. Write whatever comes to your mind, without trying to judge or organize your ideas. Write without worrying about grammar and vocabulary. At this point, you are writing to help yourself think about the topic.

2. Read what you have written. What main idea about your topic has emerged from this free writing? Write that main idea down now. Circle the parts of your free writing that support your main idea directly.

3. With your main idea in mind, reread sections of the readings that you could use in your paragraph. Take notes by paraphrasing the authors' words.

Ⓒ Expanding your point of view

1. Have a brief conference with another writer. Tell your partner (a) what your topic is, (b) what your main idea is, and (c) how you plan to support the main idea.

2. Ask your partner to summarize orally what you said to make sure you were understood.

3. Listen to your partner's impressions and suggestions. Write down thoughts and ideas that are helpful.

D Initial drafts

FIRST DRAFT

Begin your first draft with a topic sentence that expresses your main idea by narrowing the topic and making a specific statement about it. Support the topic sentence as effectively as you can. If you use an author's ideas, paraphrase them and mention the author's name.

REVISION

Put aside your first draft for a few hours or overnight. Then, before you begin revising, read the criteria listed in the *Paragraph Assessment Checklist* on page 26 at the end of this chapter. As you revise your draft, check your thinking. How clearly have you presented the topic, and how clearly have you expressed your thoughts? After you have revised your first draft, mark it "Draft 2."

E Review, revision, and assessment

PEER FEEDBACK

Read a classmate's paper and give feedback using the *Paragraph Assessment Checklist* on page 26. Write your comments on the checklist, but not on your classmate's paper. Give the checklist and the paper back to the writer. Answer any questions your classmate has about your feedback.

FURTHER REVISION

What did you learn from the feedback you received? Is your paragraph successful—is it convincing, interesting, clear, and complete? Does it sound like you? How can you change your paragraph to make it more successful?

Revise your paper using the feedback you got in class. Edit your paper for fragments. Give your teacher all your drafts, with the last marked "Final draft." Include the *Paragraph Assessment Checklist* completed by your classmate.

Writer's name: _____

Reader's name: _____

Paragraph Assessment Checklist   Chapter 1

These are the criteria for a well-written paragraph. Use them to examine your writing, or a classmate's, and check *Yes* or *No* for each item. You may wish to add comments or suggestions.

Content and ideas   Yes   No   *Reader's comments*

		Yes	No	
1	The writer has thought carefully about the topic and has a clear main idea.	❏	❏	
2	The paragraph is convincing because there are enough logical points to support the main idea.	❏	❏	
3	Only relevant points are included.	❏	❏	
4	The paper has the writer's voice; that is, it sounds like him/her.	❏	❏	

Organization and form

		Yes	No	
5	The paragraph has correct format. The first sentence is indented, and the remaining sentences follow each other without gaps.	❏	❏	
6	The main idea is clearly expressed in a topic sentence.	❏	❏	
7	The logic is easy to follow; the reader understands the paper after one reading.	❏	❏	

Language

		Yes	No	
8	The paper is easy to understand. These elements are used well:			
	• sentence structure (no fragments)	❏	❏	
	• grammar	❏	❏	
	• vocabulary	❏	❏	
	• mechanics (spelling, capitalization, punctuation)	❏	❏	

CHAPTER 2

Matters of the Heart

- How is the love between two people of a couple and the love among family members different?
- Is one kind of love stronger than the other? More important than the other?

PART 1

INTRODUCTION TO THE TOPIC, READING, AND DISCUSSION

A) Reflection

Read the statements. Decide whether each one is very accurate (*VA*), somewhat accurate (*SA*), or not accurate (*NA*) in your opinion.

_____ 1 True love is eternal; it can never die or turn into hatred.

_____ 2 It is dangerous to worship another person, that is, to love and respect that person too much.

_____ 3 The person you love should be willing to change bad habits or things that bother you.

_____ 4 It is difficult to be married to someone from a different background, that is, someone whose race, culture, religion, or world view is different from yours.

_____ 5 An older, wiser family member is probably better at choosing the right person for a young person to marry than the young person is.

_____ 6 "A good marriage is not a gift—it's an achievement." *(Ann Landers, American columnist)*

Follow-up Compare and discuss your answers with a classmate.

B) Discussion

The excerpt that follows is from "As It Was in the Beginning," a story written in the late 1800s by E. Pauline Johnson, a member of the Cree tribe of Canadian Aboriginals. The story is about Esther, a young Aboriginal woman who left her family to become educated and converted to Christianity. She has learned the white man's ways but is very homesick. She misses the more natural surroundings of her people. Read the notes and the excerpt that follow, and then discuss the questions on the next page with your classmates.

LANGUAGE NOTES

Today, Canadians refer to their native population as Aboriginals; in the United States, that population is referred to as Native Americans. The terms *Redskin* and *Indian* are no longer acceptable ways to refer to native peoples. A *tepee* is a cone-shaped home made of wooden poles and animal skins. The literal meaning of *pagan* is a person who does not follow one of the world's major religions. The connotation here is of a wild, uncivilized person. *Buckskin* is deer leather, from which Esther's tribe made their clothing at the time of the story more than 100 years ago. In those days animal skins were *tanned,* or made into leather through a process with heat, and were traded by the Aboriginals for goods at an English company, the *Hudson's Bay Company.* Father Paul is a *missionary,* a Catholic priest whose mission, or job, was to educate and convert the native people to Christianity. *Father* is his title, not his relationship to anyone in the story.

(*Note:* Words in italics are from the story.)

Read the excerpt to answer this question:

Is Esther's homesickness temporary, or will it continue after this episode?

> ... I wanted my own people, my own old life, my blood called out for it, but they always said I must not return to my father's tepee. I heard them talk amongst themselves of keeping me away from pagan influences; they told each other that if I returned to the prairies, the tepees, I would degenerate, slip back to paganism, as other girls had done; marry, perhaps, with a pagan—and all 5
> their years of labor and teaching would be lost.
>   I said nothing, but I waited. And then one night the feeling overcame me. I was in the Hudson's Bay store when an Indian came in from the north with a large pack of buckskin. As they unrolled it a dash of its insinuating odor filled the store. I went over and leaned above the skins a second, then buried my face 10
> in them, swallowing, drinking the fragrance of them, that went to my head like wine. Oh, the wild wonder of that wood-smoked tan, the subtlety of it, the untamed smell of it! I drank it into my lungs, my innermost being was saturated with it, till my mind reeled and my heart seemed twisted with a physical agony. My childhood recollections rushed upon me, devoured me. I left the store in a 15
> strange, calm frenzy, and going rapidly into the mission house I confronted my Father Paul and demanded to be allowed to go "home," if only for a day. He received the request with the same refusal and the same gentle sigh that I had so often been greeted with, but this time the desire, the smoke-tan, the heartache, never lessened. 20

 Discuss these questions in pairs or as a class.

1 Is Esther's homesickness temporary, or will it continue after this episode?

2 Is Father Paul more interested in Esther's happiness or in the success of his work? Explain.

3 What, in your opinion, can Esther do to overcome her strong feelings of homesickness?

4 How does this passage make you feel? Have you ever reacted very strongly to a familiar smell?

5 As you will read in the passage that follows, something happens one night in the story to change Esther's mind about her homesickness. What do you think happens?

ⓒ Preparing to read

NOTES ON THE READING ··

Some words in the story are specific to life of that time: *moccasins* for shoes, *lodge* for a home, and *factor* for the manager of the Hudson's Bay Company. Esther mentions her beaded bag, a small decorated leather bag used for Aboriginal folk medicine.

The author was half Cree/half English, but her story is important not simply because of its insights into Aboriginal character or life. It is important because it deals with very universal issues like homesickness, prejudice, and love. The ending of the story may surprise you.

(*Note:* Words in italics are from the reading.)

PREVIEWING THE VOCABULARY ···

Before reading, preview the vocabulary in context. Read these key sentences based on the text, and choose the best meaning for the underlined words.

1. Night after night I would steal away by myself and go to the border of the village to watch the sun set in the foothills, <u>to long and long for my father's lodge</u>.
   a. desire strongly to be in the lodge
   b. wonder how far my father's home was
   c. wait impatiently to visit my father's home

2. No more the tepees; no more the wild stretch of prairie; no more the fragrance of buckskin; no more the <u>dulcet cadence</u> of the sweet Cree tongue.
   a. sad sounds
   b. loud screams
   c. pleasant rhythm

3. Father Paul was reading evening prayers in the large room beyond the hallway; his soft, saint-like voice stole beyond the doors, like a <u>benediction</u> upon us.
   a. joyful sound
   b. a curse, asking God to punish someone
   c. a blessing, a prayer for God's good wishes

4. "Why, you can't marry this girl—no, no, sit, sit until I have finished," Father Paul said, as Laurence sprang up, <u>remonstrating</u>.
   a. crying
   b. protesting, arguing
   c. agreeing with him

5 "Her mother is hopelessly uncivilized; her father has a dash of French somewhere—half-breed, you know, my boy, half-breed."
   a. of mixed race
   b. of unknown origins
   c. of inferior intelligence

6 "She is the daughter of the Church, but you can never tell what lurks in a caged animal that has once been wild."
   a. remains
   b. is missing
   c. stays hidden, waiting to attack

7 His small old eyes were riveted on Laurence like a hawk's on a rat.
   a. looking angrily at
   b. looking away from
   c. fixed, concentrated on

8 Could those words have been spoken by my venerable teacher, whom I revered as I would one of the saints in his own black book?
   a. caring
   b. hateful
   c. deserving respect

9 Finally accepting this unpleasant idea, Laurence shuddered, lifted his face, and uttered these terrible words hoarsely: "You're right, uncle; perhaps I'd better not do this."
   a. smiled quietly
   b. laughed loudly
   c. trembled, shook

10 The news of the death will break Father Paul's heart and blight his life.
   a. destroy
   b. lengthen
   c. complicate

11 The idea wound itself about me like the very coils of a serpent.
   a. hurt me
   b. came to me quickly
   c. took control of me, surrounded me

12 Not wanting to be seen, I turned the lamp down and slipped out of the room.
   a. moved quietly
   b. walked normally
   c. moved carelessly and noisily

13 Because of the death, it was said that Father Paul was <u>bowed with grief</u>.
   a. guilty of something
   b. carrying great sadness
   c. denying he had done wrong

14 He said that <u>I was suspected</u>, but that there was no proof.
   a. I would be sorry
   b. I was the victim
   c. they thought I was guilty

Follow-up Check and discuss your answers in pairs or with the class.

D Reading for overall meaning

At this point in the story, the author introduces Laurence, Father Paul's nephew. He grew up at the mission along with Esther, with whom he attended school and played daily. They are like brother and sister.

Read the story at a quick but comfortable pace. As you read, look for the answer to this question:

Does Esther stay at the mission or return to her people?

As It Was in the Beginning

E. Pauline Johnson

Night after night I would steal away by myself and go to the border of the village to watch the sun set in the foothills, to gaze at the far line of sky and prairie, to long and long for my father's lodge. And Laurence—always Laurence—my fair-haired, laughing, child playmate, would come calling and calling for me: "Esther, where are you? We miss you; come in, Esther, come in with me." And if 5
I did not turn at once to him and follow, he would come and place his strong hands on my shoulders and laugh into my eyes and say, "Truant, truant, Esther; can't *we* make you happy?"

My old child playmate had vanished years ago. He was a tall, slender young man now, handsome as a young chief, but with laughing blue eyes, and always 10
those yellow curls around his temples. He was my solace in my half-exile, my comrade, my brother, until one night it was, "Esther, Esther, can't *I* make you happy?"

I did not answer him, only looked out across the plains and thought of the tepees. He came close, close. He locked his arms about me, and with my face 15
pressed up to his throat he stood silent. I felt the blood from my heart sweep to my very fingertips. I loved him. Oh God, how I loved him! In a wild, blind instant it all came, just because he held me so and was whispering brokenly,

continued

"Don't leave me, don't leave me, Esther; my Esther, my child love, my playmate, my girl comrade, my little Cree sweetheart, will you go away to your people, or stay, stay for me, for my arms, as I have you now?"

No more, no more the tepees; no more the wild stretch of prairie, the intoxicating fragrance of the smoke-tanned buckskin; no more the bed of buffalo hide, the soft, silent moccasin; no more the dark faces of my people, the dulcet cadence of the sweet Cree tongue—only this man, this fair, proud, tender man who held me in his arms, in his heart. My soul prayed to his great white God, in that moment, that He let me have only this. It was twilight when we re-entered the mission gate. We were both excited, feverish. Father Paul was reading evening prayers in the large room beyond the hallway; his soft, saint-like voice stole beyond the doors, like a benediction upon us. I went noiselessly upstairs to my own room and sat there undisturbed for hours. . . .

[Laurence meets Father Paul, his uncle, and tells him of his love for Esther and his desire to marry her. Father Paul is very upset. Esther overhears the conversation.]

"Laurence, my boy, your future is the dearest thing to me of all earthly interests. Why, you *can't* marry this girl—no, no, sit, sit until I have finished," he added, with a raised voice, as Laurence sprang up, remonstrating. "I have long since decided that you marry well; for instance, the Hudson's Bay factor's daughter."

Laurence broke into a fresh, rollicking laugh. "What, uncle," he said, "Little Ida McIntosh? Marry that little yellow-haired fluff ball, that kitten, that pretty little dolly?"

"Stop," said Father Paul. Then with a low, soft persuasiveness, "She is *white*, Laurence."

My lover started. "Why, uncle, what do you mean?" he faltered.

"Only this, my son: poor Esther comes of uncertain blood; would it do for you—the missionary's nephew, and adopted son, you might say—to marry the daughter of a pagan Indian? Her mother is hopelessly uncivilized; her father has a dash of French somewhere—half-breed, you know, my boy, half-breed." Then, with still lower tone and half-shut, crafty eyes, he added: "The blood is a bad, bad mixture, you know that; you know, too, that I am very fond of the girl, poor dear Esther. I have tried to separate her from evil pagan influences; she is the daughter of the Church; I want her to have no other parent; but you can never tell what lurks in a caged animal that has once been wild. My whole heart is with the Indian people, my son; my whole heart, my whole life, has been devoted to bringing them to Christ, but it is a different thing to marry with one of them."

His small old eyes were riveted on Laurence like a hawk's on a rat. My heart lay like ice in my bosom. . . .

I listened, sitting like one frozen. Could those words have been uttered by my venerable teacher, by him whom I revered as I would one of the saints in his

continued

own black book? Ah, there was no mistaking it. My white father, my life-long friend who pretended to love me, to care for my happiness, was urging the man I worshiped to forget me, to marry with the factor's daughter—because of what? Of my red skin; my good, old, honest pagan mother, my confiding French-Indian father. In a second all the care, the hollow love he had given me since my childhood, were as things that never existed. I hated that old mission priest as I hated his white man's hell. . . .

Laurence sat motionless, his face buried in his hands, but the old man continued: "No, no; not the child of the pagan mother; you can't trust her, my son. What would you do with a wife who might any day break from you to return to her prairies and her buckskins? *You can't trust her.* . . ."

Laurence shuddered, lifted his face, and said hoarsely: "You're right, uncle; perhaps I'd better not; I'll go away, I'll forget her, and then—well then—yes, you are right, it is a different thing to marry one of them."

"Good-night, son," he said.

"Good-night, uncle, and thank you for bringing me to myself."

They were the last words I ever heard uttered by either that old archfiend or his weak, miserable kinsman. . . .

What were his years of kindness and care now? What did I care for his God, his heaven, his hell? He had robbed me of my native faith, of my parents, of this last, this life of love that would have made a great, good woman of me. God, how I hated him! I crept to the closet in my dark little room. I felt for a bundle I had not looked at for years—yes, it was there, the buckskin dress I had worn as a little child when they brought me to the mission. I tucked it under my arm and descended the stairs noiselessly. I would look into the study and speak good-bye to Laurence; then I would—

I pushed open the door. He was lying on the couch where a short time previously he had sat, white and speechless, listening to Father Paul. I moved towards him softly.

God in heaven, he was already asleep. As I bent over him the fullness of his perfect beauty impressed me for the first time; his slender form, his curving mouth that almost laughed even in sleep, his fair, tossed hair, his smooth, strong-pulsing throat. God! How I loved him!

Then there arose the picture of the factor's daughter. I hated her. I hated her baby face, her yellow hair, her whitish skin. "She shall not marry him," my soul said. "I will kill him first—kill his beautiful body, his lying, false heart." Something in my heart seemed to speak; it said over and over again, "Kill him, kill him; she will never have him then. Kill him. It will break Father Paul's heart and blight his life. He has killed the best of you, of your womanhood; kill his best, his pride, his hope—his sister's son, his nephew Laurence." But how? How?

What had that terrible old man said I was like? *A strange snake.* A snake? The idea wound itself about me like the very coils of a serpent. What was this in the beaded bag of my buckskin dress? This little thing rolled in tan that my mother

continued

had given me at parting with the words, "Don't touch much, but sometime maybe you want it!" Oh! I knew well enough what it was—a small flint arrow- 105
head dipped in the venom of some strange snake.

    I knelt beside him and laid my hot lips on his hand. I worshiped him, oh, how I worshiped him! Then again the vision of her baby face, her yellow hair—I scratched his wrist twice with the arrow-tip. A single drop of red blood oozed up; he stirred. I turned the lamp down and slipped out of the room—out of the 110 house.

    I dream nightly of the horrors of the white man's hell. Why did they teach me of it, only to fling me into it?

    Last night as I crouched beside my mother on the buffalo-hide, Dan Henderson, the trapper, came in to smoke with my father. He said old Father Paul was 115 bowed with grief, that with my disappearance I was suspected, but that there was no proof. Was it not merely a snake bite?

    They account for it by the fact that I am a Redskin.

    They seem to have forgotten I am a woman.

 Follow-up Now answer this question:

    Does Esther stay at the mission or return to her people?

E Reading for more detail

Read the selection a second time. Use the questions below to read for more detail and to bring your experience to the story.

1. What ended Esther's homesickness? Do you find this quick change in her believable?

2. What ended her new happiness?

3. How did Father Paul convince Laurence? Do you agree with Father Paul's reasons?

4. After Father Paul spoke to Laurence, how did Esther's feelings for them change?

5. Did Esther really love Laurence? Father Paul? If so, did she stop loving them?

6. What solution did Esther have for the jealousy and hatred she felt? Can you understand why she acted as she did?

7. *Key words* Make a list of six words or expressions that you feel are important to the story. Be ready to explain what each word means and why it is important.

Follow-up Discuss your answers in pairs, in small groups, or as a class.

PART 2
PERSONAL WRITTEN RESPONSE

Ⓐ Journals: A private audience

Choose two of the following topics. Write for about 20 minutes in your journal notebook. Express your opinions and feelings honestly. These journal entries are for your eyes only, so do not spend a lot of time using a dictionary or worrying about grammar.

1. Which one of the three main characters do you like the most? Why?
2. Which of the three do you like the least? Why?
3. How did you feel when you finished reading the story? Were you upset? Pleased for Esther? Satisfied that she'd taken revenge? Shocked by her actions?

Ⓑ Shared writing

Choose two of the following topics to answer, and write for a total of 20 minutes. Your audience is your classmates, with whom you will share your writing. They will be interested not only in what you feel but also in why you feel that way. Express your views clearly and support them.

1. Can you understand why Esther killed Laurence? Can you accept that she did so?
2. What does Esther mean by the last two lines of the story, speaking about the murder? "They account for it by the fact that I am a Redskin. They seem to have forgotten I am a woman."
3. Do you find this story believable? Explain.

Ⓒ Feedback on your writing

Get feedback on how clear and logical your thinking and writing are. Select one of the questions from *Shared Writing,* and read your answer to a small group of classmates. Follow the *Peer Feedback Guidelines* on page 11.

PART 3
FURTHER READING, WRITING, AND DISCUSSION

A Preparing to read

NOTES ON THE READING

In this Ethiopian folktale we learn a lesson about love and about *determination* (or *resolve*), a quality that keeps us from giving up, that keeps us trying until we succeed. The couple in this tale is *overwhelmed* with problems; that is, their difficulties have become too much for them. The result is a loss of *harmony,* or peaceful relations. A wise man tells the woman that she must take something from a lion. She fears the lion's *claws* (sharp nails) and its *fangs* (long, sharp teeth).

(*Note:* Words in italics are from the folktale.)

B Reading for overall meaning

Read the folktale the first time to answer this question:

Did the old judge's medicine solve the young wife's problem?

The Lion's Hair

In a village in the mountains of Ethiopia, a young man and a young woman fell in love and became husband and wife. For a short while they were perfectly happy, but then trouble entered their house. They began to find fault with each other over little things—he blamed her for spending too much at the market, or she criticized him for always being late. It seemed not a day passed without some kind of quarrel about money or friends or household chores. Sometimes they grew so angry they shouted at each other and yelled bitter curses, and then went to bed without speaking, but that only made things worse.

After a few months, when she thought she could stand it no longer, the young wife went to a wise old judge to ask for a divorce.

"Why?" asked the old man. "You've been married barely a year. Don't you love your husband?"

"Yes, we love each other. But it's just not working out."

"What do you mean, not working out?"

"We fight a lot. He does things that bother me. He leaves his clothes lying around the house. He drops his toenails on the floor. He stays out too late. When I want to do one thing, he wants to do another. We just can't live together."

"I see," said the old man. "Perhaps I can help you. I know of a magic medicine that will make the two of you get along much better. If I give it to you, will you put aside these thoughts of divorce?"

"Yes!" cried the woman. "Give it to me."

"Wait," replied the judge. "To make the medicine, I must have a single hair from the tail of a fierce lion that lives down by the river. You must bring it to me."

"But how can I get such a hair?" the woman cried. "The lion will surely kill me."

"There I cannot help you," the old man shook his head. "I know much about making medicines, but I know little of lions. You must discover a way yourself. Can you do it?"

The young wife thought long and hard. She loved her husband very much. The magic medicine might save their marriage. She resolved to get the hair, no matter what.

continued

The very next morning she walked down to the river, hid behind some rocks, and waited. After a while, the lion came by to drink. When she saw his huge claws, she froze with fear. When he bared his sharp fangs, she nearly fainted. And when he gave his mighty roar, she turned and ran home.

But the next morning she came back, this time carrying a sack of fresh meat. She set the food on the ground, two hundred yards from the lion, and then hid behind the rocks while the lion ate.

The next day, she set the meat down one hundred yards away from the lion. And on the following morning, she put the food only fifty yards away, and stood nearby while he gulped it down.

And so every day she drew closer and closer to the fierce, wild beast. After a while she stood near enough to throw him the food, and finally came the day when she fed him right from her hand! She trembled as she watched the great teeth ripping and tearing the meat. But she loved her husband more than she feared the lion. Closing her eyes, she reached out and pulled a single hair from the tail.

Then she ran as fast as she could to the wise old judge.

"Look!" she cried. "I've brought a hair from the lion!"

The old man took the hair and looked at it closely.

"This is a brave thing you have done," he said. "It took a great deal of patience and resolve."

"Yes," said the woman. "Now give me the medicine to make my marriage better!"

The old man shook his head.

"I have nothing else to give you."

"But you promised!" the young wife cried.

"Don't you see?" asked the old man gently. "I have already given you all the medicine you need. You were determined to do whatever it took, however long it took, to gain a magic remedy for your problems. But there is no magic remedy. There is only your determination. You say you and your husband love each other. If you both give your marriage the same patience and resolve and courage you showed in getting this hair, you will be happy together for a long time. Think about it."

And so the woman went home with new resolution.

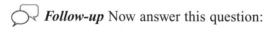 *Follow-up* Now answer this question:

Did the old judge's medicine solve the young wife's problem? Explain.

ⓒ Reading for more detail

Read the folktale again. Mark any places in the text that are still unclear to you.

D Helping each other understand

Write for about 20 minutes on one or more of the questions below.

1. What do you have trouble understanding?
2. What do you think of the old judge?
3. Do you admire the young wife?

Follow-up To a small group of students, read what you have written. Read your reaction a second time if necessary. Each group member will respond with (1) a question, (2) a comment, and/or (3) help with what you didn't understand.

E Discussion: Critical thinking

Discuss these questions in pairs, in small groups, or as a class.

1. Which character, Esther or the Ethiopian wife, loves more deeply? Explain.
2. Love doesn't seem to be as important to three of the men in these stories (Laurence, Father Paul, and the Ethiopian husband) as it is to the women. Is this the way it is in life? Do women love more strongly than men? Explain.
3. Imagine a different ending in the story of Esther and Laurence. Imagine that Father Paul does not speak to Laurence about Esther. How might the story continue? Would it end happily? Explain.

PART 4
FOCUS ON WRITING SKILLS

A Using another's writing: Summarizing

In academic courses your teachers expect you to incorporate what you have read into your own thinking and writing. In Chapter 1 you practiced paraphrasing, or expressing the author's ideas in your own words. In this chapter you will summarize, or give the main idea of, a passage from a story in a sentence or two. A summary cannot have all the details of the original, but it should have the most important ideas. To avoid plagiarism, it must be written in your own words.

EXERCISE 1 *Summarizing passages from a story*

Summarize the passages below by following these steps:

1. Read the passage two or three times.

2. Decide on the most important ideas. On a piece of paper, write down words and expressions that remind you of these essential points.

3. Expand your key words into a sentence or two. Limit your summary to 25–30 words.

Passage 1
My childhood recollections rushed upon me, devoured me. I left the store in a strange, calm frenzy, and going rapidly to the mission house I confronted my Father Paul and demanded to be allowed to go "home," if only for a day. He received the request with the same refusal and the same gentle sigh that I had so often been greeted with, but this time the desire, the smoke-tan, the heart-ache, never lessened.

<u>Key words</u>
felt homesick
begged to go home
Father Paul refused
feeling remained

<u>Summary</u>
The homesickness Esther felt was so strong that she begged to go home, but Father Paul refused. Her homesickness remained as strong as before.

Passage 2
I knelt beside him and laid my hot lips on his hand. I worshiped him, oh, how I worshiped him! Then again the vision of her baby face, her yellow hair—I scratched his wrist twice with the arrow tip. A single drop of red blood oozed up; he stirred. I turned the lamp down and slipped out of the room—out of the house.

Passage 3
In a village in the mountains of Ethiopia, a young man and a young woman fell in love and became husband and wife. For a short while they were perfectly happy, but then trouble entered their house. They began to find fault with each other over little things—he blamed her for spending too much at the market, or she criticized him for always being late. It seemed not a day passed without some kind of quarrel about money or friends or household chores.

Passage 4
And so every day she drew closer and closer to the fierce, wild beast. After a while she stood near enough to throw him the food, and finally came the day when she fed him right from her hand! She trembled as she watched the great teeth ripping and tearing the meat. But she loved her husband more than she feared the lion. Closing her eyes, she reached out and pulled a single hair from the tail.

B Meeting reader expectations: Patterns of organization

Formal English writing uses a number of different *patterns of organization*. Using patterns of organization familiar to readers will help you communicate with an English-speaking audience more effectively.

EXERCISE 2 *Model paragraphs: Patterns of organization*

The following seven paragraphs show seven common ways to develop a paragraph in English expository writing. All the paragraphs are written on the topic of jealousy. Note that some paragraphs follow more than one pattern of organization. Read each paragraph and answer the questions that follow.

Paragraph 1 *Examples*
   Literature gives us many examples of jealousy, but a look at daily life yields an ample supply closer at hand. Take the three-year-old child who lives upstairs. His parents have just brought home a newborn baby sister, and the three-year-old acts as if an enemy had entered the house. He is jealous of his sister. Or look at the wife whose husband is talking to another woman at a party. The more interested the husband seems in talking to the woman, the more unattractive and irritated his wife feels. The wife is jealous. For another example, picture a young computer programmer, considered a genius, appreciated and praised by his co-workers and boss. In comes a new programmer, who starts to share some of the attention and praise that were formerly given to the first

programmer. The first programmer feels jealous. In all three cases, the people feel their relationships threatened by a rival: They feel jealous.

1. Is there a topic sentence in which the main idea is expressed? If so, which sentence is it?
2. How many examples are used to make the writer's point? What are they?
3. Is the paragraph complete? Are there enough examples and do they make the meaning of jealousy clear? Explain.
4. If there are so "many examples of jealousy" in literature, why didn't the writer use them here? (Consider the audience.)
5. Does the author use real examples or hypothetical ones? If hypothetical, are they believable?

Paragraph 2 *Cause and effect*

An anthropological look for causes has led some experts to conclude that jealousy is biological—that it is instinctive behavior, in other words. A more interesting approach might be to look at why some people are more jealous than others. In surveys, psychologists have discovered three personality characteristics that the very jealous have in common. The first is insecurity in relationships, stemming from low self-esteem. The jealous person does not see him- or herself as worthy of the love and attention of the other person, perhaps. Another characteristic of the jealous person is a greater than normal discrepancy between how that person is and how he or she would like to be. Looking at it another way, we could say this person was quite dissatisfied with him- or herself. The last characteristic is that the very jealous tend to see worldly items such as wealth, fame, popularity, and physical attractiveness as very important. These are, of course, important to most people but not to the same degree that they are to the very jealous. That we might call these personality traits causes of jealousy is possible only because those with the characteristics exhibit abnormal levels of what is a normal human emotion, jealousy.

(Adapted from "The Heart of Jealousy," by P. Salovey and J. Rodin, Psychology Today.)

1. Is the topic sentence in the normal position as first sentence? Which is the topic sentence?
2. How many causes does the writer give? What are they?
3. How are causes different from examples?
4. Does the writer list all the causes of jealousy? Is the paragraph complete?
5. Not every paragraph has a conclusion, especially if it is part of a longer piece of writing. This paragraph has one. What is its function? Would the paragraph be as strong without it?

(*Note:* In one paragraph, it is difficult to discuss both causes and effects. As a writer, focus on one or the other as the author of paragraph 2 has done.)

Paragraph 3 *Definition*

Although a subject of many songs and much literature, jealousy is not a topic that has a long life span in most daily conversations. What is this unmentionable emotion that all people feel at times, many suffer agony over, and some are led to crime by? Jealousy is the feeling of fear, unhappiness, or even ill will that arises when a person feels that an important relationship with someone is threatened. The negative feelings are a reaction to loss—real, potential, or imagined—of someone important in our lives. Some psychologists believe that the origin of jealousy lies in biology, that is that jealousy is an instinctive response in humans. Others see an economic basis for jealousy; there is a limited amount of care a parent can give a child and a limited amount of emotional and sexual energy a spouse can give a partner. A new child in the family or a lover intrudes on these attentions. Still other theories exist to explain jealousy, the emotion difficult to talk about because it poisons the very relations that one wants to keep and nurture.

(Adapted from Jealousy: What Is It and Who Feels It?, *by Peter Van Summers, Penguin Books.)*

1. Is there a topic sentence that expresses the main idea of this paragraph? If so, what is it?

2. What definition does the writer give of jealousy?

3. To consider this paragraph one of definition, we have to look at the author's purpose in writing it. Is the purpose to make jealousy clearer by giving examples of it, as in paragraph 1 in this exercise? What is the writer's purpose?

Paragraph 4 *Comparison and contrast*

The terms *jealousy* and *envy* are often used in place of each other, but there is a basic distinction to be made between them. Envy is the feeling that we want to have something that we do not have. It could be the neighbor's car or the classmate's high score on a test. Jealousy, on the other hand, is the feeling or thought that we might lose something (more usually someone) that we already have. A jealous husband fears he will lose his wife; a jealous child fears losing a parent's love to a new sibling. If the distinction does not seem important, consider that society's reaction to the two is very different. Western society accepts jealousy but rejects envy. Westerners sympathize with the jealous lover's situation and may even secretly approve of the lover's rash actions against a rival. However, pity the person who is envious of a neighbor's swimming pool. That person is covetous* according to Western religious and cultural values and receives no sympathy.

covetous: *having a strong desire to possess something that belongs to someone else*

1. What is the topic sentence? Is the writer's purpose to compare (show similarities) or to contrast (show differences)?

2. What examples are used here? If this is a comparison/contrast paragraph, why are there examples?

3. In what two ways are jealousy and envy different?

4. There are two ways to organize a comparison/contrast paragraph: you can (1) discuss the items being compared point by point with each other, or (2) discuss one item completely and then the second item completely (often in separate paragraphs). How did this writer organize the paragraph?

5. There is no conclusion in this paragraph. Write one.

Paragraph 5 *Narrative*

   The first time I remember feeling jealous was many years ago when I was three or four. I had been carefully choosing the right crayons to color pictures in a new coloring book on the floor in the dining room. Satisfied that I had done a good job, I wanted to show my new masterpieces to my mother, who was busy with morning chores in the kitchen. My father, too, might like the pictures, but I thought he was sleeping. So into the kitchen I went carrying the new pictures. I found my mother there, but to my dismay, she was not waiting to "ooh" and "aah" at my artwork. Instead, she was in the arms of my father, who was kissing her. My attempt to interrupt this nonsense was met by, "We're busy, can't you see?" from my father. There was no response from that woman—that woman who preferred him to me, that nonsense to my masterpieces. I ran to my room brokenhearted.

1. Narration tells a story by carefully choosing details to make a point. Does this paragraph paint a picture of jealousy that you understand?

2. Is there a topic sentence here? If so, which sentence is it?

3. Which detail (or sentence) does not seem particularly relevant to the paragraph? Can it be omitted? Why or why not?

4. A narrative is organized with the events in chronological order, or the order in which they happened. Without looking at the paragraph, can you retell the events of this narrative paragraph in order?

Paragraph 6 *Description*

   John had no idea what to do about his feelings. He was ashamed of himself for how he felt when his wife spoke to another man, even the mail carrier or a clerk at the store. He could feel his anger building, like a bomb about to explode. Underneath the anger was an emptiness, a feeling that perhaps there was nothing in him to love. Were other men better looking than he was? Somehow more attractive to his wife? He couldn't actually talk to her about it because she would think he was silly for feeling jealous. More often, he would just turn away so that she couldn't read the jealousy in his eyes. The one time he had confronted her with his feelings, she didn't know what he was talking about. And when she had found him snooping in her purse (was he looking for a telltale note or some sign of another lover?), her reaction was a soft sigh of disbelief and then a look of confusion. Could he end this agony before it ended his marriage?

1. At first glance, this description might seem like a narrative paragraph. How is it different from a narrative?

2. There is no topic sentence in this paragraph, but certainly there is a main idea. Write out the main idea in your own words.

3. In description, details "paint a picture" that convey the writer's message. Good descriptive details often appeal to the senses of sight, hearing, smell, and feeling. What details does this writer use to describe a jealous person? Which ones appeal to the senses?

4. Write a topic sentence for this paragraph, one that leads the reader to expect a description.

Paragraph 7 *Classification*

Though the basic feelings involved in jealousy may be the same no matter what the cause, it can be useful to look at the different faces jealousy can wear. All cases of jealousy probably fall into one of four categories. The first, the one that probably pops into most people's minds when jealousy is brought up, is sexual jealousy, the jealousy between husband and wife or between lovers. Another kind of jealousy, found within the family unit, is jealousy among brothers and sisters. All children, with the possible exception of the youngest, have probably felt this kind of sibling rivalry. Professional jealousy is yet another kind of jealousy. Here we are talking not only about the jealousy that can exist among employees in relation to their boss or coworkers but also about the jealousy that often exists between athletes on the same team or students in the same class. Last, and perhaps the least apparent to many people, is jealousy between friends, which develops when one friend feels threatened by another friend's other friendships. This kind of jealousy or possessiveness would even include a husband who feels jealous because much of his wife's time and affection for him is now going to a new baby. That we even attempt to classify jealousy is not to imply that the jealous feeling is different in people from one classification to another. Rather, how a jealous person might try to deal with the jealousy is very likely influenced by its classification.

1. On the surface a classification paragraph can seem like an example paragraph. What differences are there between the two?

2. A good classification should account for all possible occurrences of the thing being classified. Can you think of a type of jealousy that does not fit into the four categories named above? Can you think of a better way to classify jealousy?

3 If the first sentence is not the topic sentence, how does it function in the paragraph? Which sentence is the topic sentence?

4 Look at the last two sentences. Does this paragraph need such a long conclusion? If you find the conclusion too long, rewrite it in a shorter form.

C Sentence grammar: Correcting run-on sentences

RUN-ON SENTENCES

Look at the sentences below. Can you identify the errors?

a. Communication, forgiveness, and honesty are essential to love jealousy and a lack of trust will destroy a loving relationship.

b. The Ethiopian wife we read about in *The Lion's Hair* showed patience and determination, in the other story, Esther's love was destroyed by her jealousy of Laurence.

Both sentences are *run-on sentences*. They each contain two independent clauses that are joined together improperly.

In example *a,* two independent clauses are joined together with no punctuation or conjunction. This type of run-on is called a *fused* sentence.

In example *b,* two independent clauses are separated by a comma alone. Commas are often used when we combine sentences with a coordinating conjunction, but a comma alone cannot join two independent clauses. This type of run-on is called a *comma splice*.

EXERCISE 3 *Recognizing run-on sentences*

Each of the following sentences contains two clauses. In the blank write *RO* for a run-on sentence or *C* for a correctly punctuated sentence.

_____ 1 Good communication is an essential quality of a loving relationship it doesn't matter whether the relationship is between two spouses, a parent and child, other relatives, or friends.

_____ 2 Another quality most of us look for is affection; here we are not speaking of romance or sex but caring, understanding, respect, and kindness.

_____ 3 Compassion and forgiveness, two other important qualities, cause a person to have understanding, to forgive, and to be supportive, in other words, they are qualities that lead a person to be less selfish and more selfless.

_____ 4 Honesty means a person can express his or her true feelings, and it also means the person speaks openly about fears, hopes, and expectations.

_____ 5 Acceptance means that we love the other person the way he or she is; in other words, we don't try to change the person to please ourselves.

_____ 6 Other important qualities are dependability and a sense of humor patience and freedom are two more.

(The sentences in Exercises 3–7 are adapted from Loving Each Other, *by Leo Buscaglia, Holt, Rinehart and Winston.)*

GUIDELINES FOR CORRECTING RUN-ON SENTENCES

Guideline 1
If the two independent clauses of a run-on sentence are closely related and not too long, they can be separated with a semicolon (;).

    a. Communication, forgiveness, and honesty are essential to love; jealousy and a lack of trust will destroy a loving relationship.

However, it is better to separate two longer or unrelated independent clauses with periods.

    b. The Ethiopian wife we read about in *The Lion's Hair* showed patience and determination. In the other story, Esther's love was destroyed by her jealousy.

Guideline 2
If the two independent clauses in a run-on sentence are longer, they can be separated by a period and a transition word.

    a. The Ethiopian wife we read about in *The Lion's Hair* showed patience and determination. *However,* in the other story, Esther's love was destroyed by her jealousy.

If the two independent clauses are closely related and not too long, the transition word may be preceded by a semicolon (;) instead of a period.

    b. Communication, forgiveness, and honesty are essential to love. *However,* jealousy and a lack of trust will destroy a loving relationship.

    c. Communication, forgiveness, and honesty are essential to love; *however,* jealousy and a lack of trust will destroy a loving relationship.

(*Note:* Transition words include *nevertheless, in addition, for example, moreover, therefore, consequently, also, on the other hand, in contrast, however, in other words, otherwise.*)

EXERCISE 4 *Separating run-on sentences*

Follow Guideline 1 to separate the two independent clauses and correct the run-on sentence errors. Rewrite the sentences. Use a semicolon if the clauses seem closely related; otherwise, it is better to use a period to separate them.

1 Communication does not happen only through words it happens through actions and gestures, too.

2 A compliment usually communicates appreciation criticism can be destructive.

3 Communicating with another includes admitting when you feel low or lonely not sharing these feelings creates distance.

4 It is important to accept what another says as significant and real it may not seem important to you but probably is to the speaker.

5 Sometimes good communication means respecting another's silence we must accept that people sometimes need quiet to solve problems.

EXERCISE 5 *Using transition words*

Identify the two independent clauses in each run-on sentence. Then separate the two clauses following Guideline 2. Choose the better of the two transition words shown in parentheses. Rewrite each item as one sentence with a semicolon or as two sentences separated by a period.

1 Some people feel that total honesty is essential in a loving relationship others feel it is dangerous to be completely honest. *(however / therefore)*

2 One writer feels that good lies lead to a good marriage a person should lie in order not to hurt the spouse's feelings. *(however / in other words)*

3 Another writer recommends always telling the truth trust is created between the two spouses. *(in this way / for example)*

4 Sometimes a small lie can have serious consequences a husband who tells his wife he likes a meal that he hates may end up eating that meal over and over again. *(meanwhile / for example)*

5 Eventually, the lying husband will probably explode in anger, he may say something very hurtful about his wife's cooking. *(first of all / then)*

6 Perhaps the simple truth, told tactfully in the beginning, would have been better, the wife would not have made the problem meal again. *(thus / in other words)*

7 The problem of honesty in relationships applies to all of us almost every time we speak it is an issue that is worth thinking about. *(therefore / however)*

_____

_____

Guideline 3
A coordinating conjunction *(and, but, so, nor, for, yet, or)* can be used to join two independent clauses that are closely related. When using a coordinating conjunction to join two independent clauses, place a comma before it, as in the example below.

> Communication, forgiveness, and honesty are essential to love, *but* jealousy and a lack of trust will destroy a loving relationship.

EXERCISE 6 *Using coordinating conjunctions*

Identify the two independent clauses in each run-on sentence. Then join the two clauses according to Guideline 3.

1 There are two qualities that are destructive to a loving relationship, not surprisingly, they are the opposite aspects of the essential qualities we have already looked at.

2 Lack of communication is at the top of the "destructive" list we can see how important communication is to a healthy loving relationship.

3 Selfishness can eventually destroy a loving relationship an unforgiving nature can make love disappear very quickly.

4 A lack of trust is a problem distrust can weaken any relationship.

5 A perfectionist can make the other person feel incompetent the other person may feel it is pointless trying to please the perfectionist.

Guideline 4
A subordinating conjunction *(because, although, since, whereas, so that)* can be used to join two clauses. If the dependent clause with the subordinating conjunction comes first, separate it from the independent clause with a comma. If the dependent clause comes after the independent clause, do not use a comma.

> a. The old judge devised a plan *so that* the Ethiopian wife would learn a valuable lesson about determination.
>
> b. *So that* the Ethiopian wife would learn a valuable lesson about determination, the old judge devised a plan.
>
> c. *Even though* most people realize the importance of communication, forgiveness, and honesty in life, many relationships lack these qualities.
>
> d. Many relationships lack communication, forgiveness, and honesty *even though* most people realize the importance of these qualities in life.

EXERCISE 7 *Using subordinating conjunctions*

Identify the two independent clauses in each item. Then combine them following Guideline 4. Choose from these subordinating conjunctions: *because, even though, if, unless.* You may use some words more than once.

1 Acceptance and a sense of humor aren't the qualities most people think of first they are very important qualities in a loving relationship.
2 We really love someone it means we love the person as they are, not as we would like them to be.
3 Not everything in life turns out the way we want a sense of humor about life is a way of accepting what comes our way.
4 A sense of humor can make us feel rich and happy it is not the result of how many possessions we have.
5 Some people take themselves and life too seriously they can become easily disappointed when things turn out differently than they expect.
6 We can say that we see the humor in life we are quick to laugh at ourselves and the difficulties life brings.
7 A relationship can become boring and predictable the people in the relationship have a sense of humor.

EXERCISE 8 *Editing for run-on sentences*

Edit this paragraph. First, use a slash (/) to separate the run-on sentences into two clauses. Then rewrite the paragraph, correcting the run-on sentences. Follow Guidelines 1–4. Try to use as many different guidelines as you can. Some run-on sentences can be corrected in more than one way.

Some people are probably more successful in their relationships they have the qualities essential to loving relationships. The lack of these qualities is probably the cause of many problems we have with other people many of us would benefit from developing those qualities we don't have. For example, many people get married and divorced over and over again, others don't get along with coworkers on the job. Perhaps their lives would be easier if they were better at communication if they were more honest about their feelings.

PART 5
FORMAL WRITING ASSIGNMENT

A Writing topics

Choose a writing topic from the list below. For your formal writing assignment, you will develop a paragraph on the topic you choose.

1. *Definition* Write your definition of *love*.

2. *Cause and effect* Many marriages end in divorce, often because love has failed. What are the causes of this failure? (Think in general terms, not of one particular couple you know.)

3. *Comparison and contrast* Who love more deeply—men or women? (Either concentrate on one gender in your paragraph, or write two separate paragraphs.)

4. *Narrative* Tell a story that illustrates love or the lack of it. Use chronological order. Make sure the story has a point; make that point clear in your topic sentence.

5. *Description* Describe a loving couple you know whose relationship is an example to others.

B Generating ideas: Free writing

Follow these steps for free writing.

1. Write freely for 15 or 20 minutes on your topic. Write whatever comes to mind at this point. Don't sit and ponder; write. The act of writing usually leads to more thinking about a topic.

2. Read what you have written. Circle ideas and sentences that seem especially good to you. Write down three questions that remain in your mind about the topic.

C Expanding your point of view: Group discussion

Get together with a small group of students who chose the same topic. Take turns reading your writing aloud and discussing your ideas. Write down any new ideas that come out of your discussion.

D Initial drafts

FIRST DRAFT

If a main idea has emerged in your free writing and discussion, develop it into a topic sentence. If no main idea has emerged, reread your free writing, and think about your discussions with classmates. Formulate a topic sentence to guide your writing of the paragraph.

Keep your purpose for writing in mind as you develop your topic and choose your support. Are you trying to define, compare, list causes, describe, or tell a story?

REVISION

Put aside your paragraph for an hour or two, or overnight. Then look at it again with fresh eyes. As you revise your first draft, ask yourself the questions below. When you finish revising, mark your draft "Draft 2."

1 How will others react to my writing? (Read the criteria listed in the *Paragraph Assessment Checklist* on page 54.)

2 Does it sound like I wrote this or like a stranger wrote it? (Give your paragraph your voice by writing your own thoughts, using your own examples, and keeping your audience in mind as you write. Your goal is to let your audience get to know you and your thinking better, not to impress them.)

E Review, revision, and assessment

PEER FEEDBACK

Read a classmate's paper, and give feedback using the *Paragraph Assessment Checklist* on page 54. Write your comments on the checklist, but make no marks on your classmate's paper. Give the checklist and the paper back to the writer. Answer any questions your classmate has about your feedback.

FURTHER REVISION

What did you learn from the feedback you received? Is your paragraph successful—is it convincing, interesting, clearly organized, and complete? If not, how can you make it more successful?

Revise your paper using the feedback you got in class. Give your teacher all drafts (with the last draft marked "Final draft") and the *Paragraph Assessment Checklist* completed by your classmate.

Writer's name: _____

Reader's name: _____

Paragraph Assessment Checklist   Chapter 2

These are the criteria for a well-written paragraph. Use them to examine your writing, or a classmate's, and check *Yes* or *No* for each item. You may wish to add comments or suggestions.

Content and ideas

		Yes	No	Reader's comments
1	The writer has thought carefully about the topic and has a clear main idea.	☐	☐	
2	The writer's purpose (to define, compare, or describe, and so on) is clear in the paragraph.	☐	☐	
3	The paragraph is convincing because there are enough logical points to support the main idea.	☐	☐	
4	The paper has the writer's voice; that is, it sounds like him/her.	☐	☐	

Organization and form

5	The paragraph has correct format. The first sentence is indented, and the remaining sentences follow each other without gaps.	☐	☐	
6	The main idea is clearly expressed in a topic sentence.	☐	☐	
7	The logic is easy to follow, so the reader understands the paper easily after one reading.	☐	☐	

Language

8	The paper is easy to understand. These elements are used well:			
	• sentence structure (no fragments or run-on sentences)	☐	☐	
	• grammar	☐	☐	
	• vocabulary	☐	☐	
	• mechanics (spelling, capitalization, punctuation)	☐	☐	

CHAPTER 3

Friendship

- Do you think it is important for people to be of the same sex in order to have a true friendship? Must they be the same age?
- Is it important for friends to share similar interests and backgrounds?

PART 1

INTRODUCTION TO THE TOPIC, READING, AND DISCUSSION

A Reflection

Read these quotations about friendship. Which ones make the most sense to you? Which don't make sense? Why?

1 "A false friend is more dangerous than an open enemy." *(Francis Bacon, British essayist, philosopher, and statesman)*

2 "Friendship always benefits; love sometimes injures." *(Seneca, Roman philosopher, writer)*

3 "My best friend is the man who in wishing me well wishes it for my sake."* *(Aristotle, Greek philosopher)*

4 "Your friend is the man who knows all about you, and still likes you." *(Elbert Hubbard, American author)*

for my sake: *to help me, for my benefit*

Follow-up Discuss your answers with a classmate.

B Discussion

Read these results from a survey on friendship done by the popular magazine *Psychology Today*. Put a check (✓) by statements that you find believable. Put an exclamation point (!) by statements that surprise you. Then discuss your reactions in small groups. In general, does your group find these statements believable or surprising? Why?

_____ 1 Loyalty, warmth, and the ability to keep confidences are the qualities most valued in a friend; age, income, and occupation are less important.

_____ 2 Feeling betrayed or deceived by a friend is one of the main reasons for ending a friendship.

_____ 3 In a crisis, 51 percent of the survey respondents say they would turn first to friends, not family.

_____ 4 Twenty-nine percent say they have a close friendship with someone who is a homosexual.

_____ 5 Only 26 percent think career success interferes with friendship opportunities.

56   Chapter 3

_____ 6 Seventy-three percent agree that friendships with the opposite sex are different from those with the same sex.

_____ 7 Thirteen percent would lie for a friend in a divorce proceeding.

C Preparing to read

NOTES ON THE READING

"The Friendship Bond," a report on the *Psychology Today* friendship questionnaire, commands attention because it reports answers from a large number (40,000) of respondents. The writing style is somewhat scientific in that the author reports the results of her research by giving us the statistics to support the conclusions she makes. To help us understand the reasons for her research, she presents the theories about friendship, that is, what social critics believe about friendship in the United States. Be careful to make a distinction between this theory and the writer's findings; her data, or information, may contradict or disagree with the theory.

PREVIEWING THE VOCABULARY

Before reading, preview the vocabulary in context. Read these key sentences based on the selection, and choose the best meanings for the underlined words.

1 Unlike marriage or the ties that bind parents and children, friendship appears to be a unique form of <u>bonding</u>.
   a. responsibility
   b. relationship by law
   c. feeling that brings people together

2 Social critics expect people to be dissatisfied with their friendships; the research <u>gives cold comfort to the critics</u>, however.
   a. is ignored by the critics
   b. shows the critic are correct
   c. is unwelcome news to the critics

3 Unlike other social roles we play as citizens and employees, friendship has its own rationale: to <u>enhance</u> feelings of warmth, trust, love, and affection between two people.
   a. improve
   b. decrease
   c. eliminate

4 Social critics have pointed to the <u>dislocation</u> and isolation that they think grows out of the high mobility rate among Americans and a loss of community supports.
   a. trouble using a map
   b. disregard for traditions
   c. feeling that life is out of order

5. Sociologists have described the impersonality and <u>anomie</u> of life in modern cities, where increasing numbers of people choose to live alone.
   a. feelings of hopelessness and loneliness
   b. chances for more friends
   c. opportunities for more to do

6. Because increasing numbers of people choose to live alone, critics have written a good deal about a trend toward <u>self-indulgence</u> and lack of <u>commitment</u> in our society.
   a. talking to oneself / people to talk to
   b. feeling very lonely all the time / close families
   c. doing whatever one wants / willingness to give time, energy

7. These questions provide clues as to whether people today find <u>deficits</u> in their friendships. Researchers looked for signs of dissatisfaction with the quality of people's friendships, but found few.
   a. surprises
   b. lack of something necessary
   c. conflicts with family obligations

8. When asked, for example, whether they felt that many of their friendships are not completely <u>reciprocal</u>, almost 60 percent answered no. Most obviously feel they get as much as they give in their relationships.
   a. unequal
   b. advantageous
   c. giving and receiving in return

9. Helping out a friend and turning to a friend for help <u>presuppose</u> a certain amount of trust.
   a. imagine
   b. require; assume
   c. make unnecessary

10. Social psychologists have proposed <u>a link</u> between trust and liking that seems to fit the data.
    a. a connection
    b. an impossible combination
    c. a theory that proves the existence of something

11. The rules of friendship involve the right to ask for help; presumably, the obligation to help a friend is <u>implicitly acknowledged</u>.
    a. not usually true
    b. sometimes impossible to do
    c. understood without discussion

12 Only 10 percent of the sample said they thought a friend should help another commit suicide if the friend wanted to but was too <u>feeble</u> to do it alone.

a. weak

b. crazy

c. emotional

13 In short, there is no striking <u>contradiction</u> between people's descriptions of actual friendships and their beliefs about friendship in general.

a. agreement

b. relationship

c. lack of agreement

Follow-up Check and discuss your answers in pairs or with the class.

D Reading for overall meaning

Read the selection at a quick but comfortable pace. Then answer this question:

Is the idea of friendship alive and well, or is friendship in trouble according to the study? Explain.

The Friendship Bond

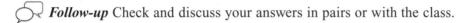

Mary Brown Parlee

More than 40,000 readers told us what they looked for in close friendships, what they expected of friends, what they were willing to give in return, and how satisfied they were with the quality of their friendships. The results give cold comfort to social critics.

Friendship appears to be a unique form of human bonding. Unlike marriage or the ties that bind parents and children, it is not defined or regulated by law. Unlike other social roles that we are expected to play—as citizens, employees, members of professional societies and other organizations—it has its own subjective rationale, which is to enhance feelings of warmth, trust, love, and affection between two people.

The questionnaire on friendship appeared in the March issue of *Psychology Today*. The findings confirm that issues of trust and betrayal are central to friendship. They also suggest that our readers do not look for friends only among those who are most like them, but find many who differ in race, sexual preference, religion, and ethnic background. Arguably the most important conclusion that emerges from the data, however, is not something that we found—but what we did not.

Social critics have pointed to the dislocation and isolation that they think grows out of the high mobility rate among Americans and a loss of community

continued

supports. Ever since the work of sociologist Emile Durkheim, they have described the impersonality and anomie of life in modern cities, where increasing numbers of people choose to live alone. They have written a good deal about a trend toward self-indulgence and lack of commitment in our society, which could very well lead to tensions in friendships just as it may be contributing to the divorce rate among married couples.

In the questionnaire responses, we looked for signs of dissatisfaction with the quality of people's friendships, but we found few. Do people confide in their friends these days? Do they tend to turn to them in times of emotional crises? Do friends become more important as one gets older? Turned around, all of these questions provide clues as to whether people today find deficits in their friendships. Most of the responses to our survey strongly suggest they do not. When asked, for example, whether they felt that many of their friendships are not completely reciprocal, almost 60 percent answered no. At least among our readers and others like them, friendship in America appears to be in sound health.

When we asked our readers to tell us what qualities they believe to be important in a friend, they valued, above all, loyalty and the ability to keep confidences. Warmth, affection, and supportiveness were also high on the list, while external characteristics such as age, income, and occupation, were not. Again, in the letters commenting on friendship in general, similar themes recurred: typical words and phrases were *trust, honesty, accepts me even when he doesn't totally approve, supportive,* and *understanding.*

Some insights into what holds friendships together can be gained from looking at what drives them apart. When asked about reasons for a friendship's cooling off or ending, readers gave as the two most important reasons feeling betrayed by a friend, and discovering that a friend had very different views on issues the respondent felt were important. The questionnaire answers thus confirm what many readers said explicitly in their comments: in a satisfying friendship, trust and feeling accepted are two of the most essential components.

Activities of Friendship

Given the importance of trust, it is not surprising that "had an intimate talk" is the activity most or second-most frequently mentioned by both men and women as something they have done with friends in the past month. Two other items high on the list of activities also presuppose a certain amount of trust and involvement: helping out a friend and turning to a friend for help.

Social psychologists have proposed a link between trust and liking that seems to fit these friendship data. The theory suggests that trust encourages self-disclosure (revealing aspects of yourself that are both precious and vulnerable). If self-disclosure meets with continued acceptance (not necessarily the same as approval of the feelings or actions), liking and affection deepen—as

continued

well as trust. In this theory, self-disclosure and trust must be reciprocated in order for the relationship to deepen.

Rules of Friendship

In addition to inquiring about actual activities, we asked some specific questions about what people would or would not do with friends, both in general and in certain hypothetical situations. We wanted our survey to give us an idea of some of the "rules" that govern, or perhaps define, behavior between friends.

As both theory and the data suggest, one rule of friendship is that friends confide in each other, sharing intimate aspects of their personal lives and feelings. Perhaps most significantly, bad as well as good news can be shared. Even though in our society, one's success is often equated with success at work, 89 percent of our sample said they would tell a close friend about a failure at work.

Furthermore, over two-thirds (68 percent) said that if they had a terminal illness, they would tell a friend. Eighty-seven percent of the respondents say they talk with friends about sexual activities (60 percent discussing activities in general, 27 percent in detail).

Our respondents clearly indicated that in some situations, the rules of friendship involve the right to ask for help (presumably the obligation to help a friend is also implicitly acknowledged). When asked who they would turn to first in a crisis, over half (51 percent) said they would turn to friends before family. This was true for all subgroups, even though older people in the sample said they tend to rely more on family and professional counselors in a crisis than do the younger age groups, and a higher proportion of men than women said they go it alone.

Yet friendship has limits. Only 10 percent of the sample said they thought a friend should help another commit suicide if the friend wanted to but was too feeble to do it alone (41 percent said no and 36 percent were opposed to suicide.)

In short, there are no striking contradictions between people's descriptions of actual friendships, their beliefs about friendship in general, and their perception of the rules that apply to these relationships. This consistency, and the enthusiastic descriptions of friends and friendship we received, suggest that our readers are satisfied with their friendships, even though 67 percent of the respondents also acknowledge feeling lonely "sometimes" or "often."

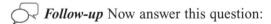 *Follow-up* Now answer this question:

> *Is the idea of friendship alive and well, or is friendship in trouble according to the study? Explain.*

E Reading for more detail

Read the article a second time. Use the questions below to read for more detail and to bring your experience to the reading.

1 Why did social critics expect people to be dissatisfied with their friendships? In what way were the critics' expectations wrong?

2 What five qualities did people say were most important to them in a friend? Would you list the same five qualities? In the same order?

3 What are the two reasons given for ending a friendship? Which of the two reasons makes more sense to you?

4 What three activities are most characteristic among friends in this survey? What role does trust play in these activities?

5 What two rules of friendship do the respondents mention? Do you follow the same rules with your friends?

6 What limits do the respondents put on friendship? Can you be good friends with someone and say no to him or her?

7 *Key words* Make a list of six words or expressions that you feel are important to the reading. Be ready to explain what each word means and why it is important.

Follow-up Compare and discuss your answers in pairs, small groups, or as a class.

PART 2
PERSONAL WRITTEN RESPONSE

Ⓐ Journals: A private audience

Choose two of the following topics. Write for about 20 minutes in your journal notebook. Express your opinions and feelings honestly. These journal entries are for your eyes only, so do not spend a lot of time using a dictionary or worrying about grammar.

1. Who is your closest friend? What makes the two of you close?
2. Can friends ever be more important to you than family?
3. Who has hurt you more in your life—a friend or a relative?

Ⓑ Shared writing

Choose two of the following topics, and write for a total of 20 minutes. Your audience is your classmates, with whom you will share your writing. They will be interested not only in what you feel but also in why you feel that way. Express your views clearly and support them.

1. How important is it to confide in a friend? Can you be friends with someone without revealing parts of yourself?
2. Have you ever had any fair-weather friends, that is, people who stop being your friend when you are in trouble? Explain.
3. Have you ever ended a friendship? If so, why?

Ⓒ Feedback on your writing

Get feedback on how clear and logical your thinking and writing are. Select one of the questions from *Shared Writing,* and read your answer to a small group of classmates. Follow the *Peer Feedback Guidelines* on page 11.

PART 3

FURTHER READING, WRITING, AND DISCUSSION

A Preparing to read

NOTES ON THE READING

This selection from a newspaper tells a true story about two women from different backgrounds who taught together in a school. The writer mentions the *rift*—the serious disagreement or division—between her culture and that of her fellow teacher. She compares their relationship to the one between the Montagues and Capulets, two warring families in Shakespeare's *Romeo and Juliet.* In this story the writer *falls out of favor* with the administration at her school, meaning that they no longer like her. Therefore, she feels like a *pariah,* a person not accepted by anyone. Unfortunately, it seems she has no *allies,* or friends, to help and support her.

   (*Note:* Words in italics are from the selection.)

B Reading for overall meaning

Read the essay the first time to answer this question:

Did the two women in the essay merely act like friends, or did they become real friends?

Heart Speaks to Heart Across a Cultural Divide

Gail Saunders

She taught me about friendship, even though a friendship between us seemed unlikely. But then, a friendship between people from different backgrounds always is. Our cultures are longstanding enemies, the Montagues and the Capulets of our part of the world, distant cousins separated by a centuries-old rift.

We were working together as teachers, and it was our first year at that school. We happened to be neighbors, too. Our rooms were right across from one another, separated by only a strip of tar and some stones and debris that had missed old, dented garbage cans.

At first we were cordial with each other, the way co-workers are supposed to be. We often made small talk about our aides, a memo sent, our kids. It was pleasant, but I felt there was a barrier and that the wall of political and ideological differences would separate us forever.

I could be polite, though, even if she just didn't seem to get it. We only had to work together. It didn't mean that we had to be friends; we just had to peacefully coexist. "Hello, how are you?" and "I'm fine" was about as far as it was going to go. That was fine with me.

Then one day, I fell out of favor with the school administration. It began as something very small, an argument with a co-worker, and it grew into something very big. I was called into a meeting and told that perhaps I would be happier working somewhere else. The woman with whom I'd had the conflict wasn't leaving, they said, so I had to. They said many ugly and untrue things. My feelings were hurt. I stopped smiling at people. I withdrew and stopped socializing. I felt like a pariah, someone that people were whispering about.

My neighbor, separated by a strip of tar and a centuries-old rift, my people's bitter and sworn enemy, caught my eye one day in the cafeteria, and I knew that she knew.

"It's as though someone took the life out of you," she said. "You are like a different person, and it hurts my heart to see you like that."

From then on, we began taking long walks together during our conference

continued

periods, which happened to coincide. We would talk about what had happened. She gently upbraided me for my actions, at first. "You needed allies," she said. "Then this wouldn't have happened."

"It could have happened to anyone," I countered, "even you." She agreed, and she continued to take my side.

Sometimes she would confide to me about the wrongs and slights she had also suffered at work. Sometimes she would bring a dish that she had made at home, and we would sit down and eat together and talk about our philosophies on life, our religions, our families.

Not that we didn't have our differences. We did. At times she made comments that I thought were boastful.

"Do I dare say something to her about it," I thought, "and risk alienating the one person who has been my friend and really cares?" In the end, I did say something, and my friend listened patiently. As it turned out, some of our differences were cultural, and her explanations brought us even closer together— my bitter and sworn enemy.

She stuck by me and stayed to help pick up the pieces when no one else did; others were too busy, or didn't care.

And in the end, my friend and I began to see over the top of the wall of our political and cultural differences. We exchanged phone numbers. And on my goodbye card, she simply wrote, "To my best friend: I wish you the best."

Follow-up Now answer this question:

Did the two women in the essay merely act like friends, or did they become real friends?

C Reading for more detail

Read the selection again. Mark any places in the text that are still unclear to you.

D Helping each other understand

Write for about 20 minutes on one or more of the questions below.

1 What do you have trouble understanding in the essay?

2 Have you ever have been in a situation like the author's, where you really needed a friend?

3 Have you had a similarly improbable or unlikely friendship?

Follow-up To a small group of students, read what you have written. Each group member will respond with (1) a question, (2) a comment, and/or (3) help with what you didn't understand.

E Discussion: Critical thinking

Discuss these questions in pairs, in small groups, or as a class.

1 Relatives can be friends, but friends do not usually become relatives. Can friends be as important to you as relatives? Explain.

2 Can you be as good friends with someone from another culture as with someone from your own culture? Explain.

3 English has two contradictory sayings that can apply to friendship: "Birds of a feather flock together," and "Opposites attract." What do they mean? Which saying describes friendship more accurately in your experience?

4 Do women make friends more easily than men do? Do they know how to be better friends than men do? Explain.

PART 4
FOCUS ON WRITING SKILLS

A Using another's writing: More on paraphrasing

In your formal writing assignment in this chapter, you may want to use some of the authors' ideas. Do so, but be sure to put their ideas into your own words by paraphrasing.

EXERCISE 1 *More practice in paraphrasing sentences*

Read each sentence below, and find it in the first reading selection, "The Friendship Bond." Read the context (the lines before and after) of the sentence several times. Then paraphrase the sentence in your own words. To avoid using the author's wording, change the structure of the original sentence, and do not use the italicized words in your paraphrase. Finally, revise your sentence to make sure your paraphrase is clear and grammatical.

1 "Unlike marriage or the ties that *bind* parents and children, it is not defined or regulated by law." (lines 5–6)

> Paraphrase: The law defines relationships between spouses and between parents and children and tells us how to act in them; it does not do the same for friendship.
>
> Revision: The law clearly states what family relationships are and how we should act in them; it does not do the same for friendships.

2 "The findings confirm that *issues* of trust and betrayal are *central* to friendship." (lines 12–13)

3 "The questionnaire answers thus *confirm* what many readers said explicitly in their comments: in a *satisfying* friendship, trust and feeling accepted are two of the most essential components." (lines 47–50)

4 "In short, there are no striking *contradictions* between people's descriptions of actual friendships, their *beliefs* about friendship in general, and their *perception* of the rules that apply to these relationships." (lines 89–91)

Follow-up Exchange and compare paraphrases with at least one other student. What are the differences in your paraphrases?

B Meeting reader expectations: The essay and logical assertions

A good English paragraph expresses one main idea and provides the reader with enough logical support to be convincing. We can look at an essay the same way, with one difference: The main idea is more general, so it needs more discussion and support. Traditionally, an academic essay has four or more paragraphs, which correspond in function to the three parts of the paragraph.

Look at this comparison between the parts of a paragraph and the parts of an essay:

The Parts of a Paragraph	The Parts of an Essay
1 *Topic sentence* Expresses the main idea of a paragraph in a sentence.	***Introduction paragraph and thesis statement*** Typically, the introduction begins in a general way and moves logically toward the thesis statement, which expresses the main idea of the essay in a sentence. The thesis statement is often the last sentence in this first paragraph.
2 *Points of support (1, 2, 3, etc.)* More specific ideas that support the topic sentence.	***Body paragraphs (1, 2, 3, etc.)*** Each body paragraph will have its own main idea and therefore its own topic sentence. But each paragraph will support the thesis statement directly.
3 *Conclusion* One sentence, often found in longer paragraphs.	***Conclusion paragraph*** An essay needs a conclusion to end effectively. The concluding sentences move from the specific (the thesis of the essay) back to something more general, such as friendship or life.

EXERCISE 2 *Parts of the essay*

Read the sentences on the following page carefully. They are all from an essay on friendship. Decide how each one might function in the full essay:

- as the thesis statement
- as a topic sentence of a body paragraph
- as part of the conclusion

Place the letter of each sentence where it fits in the essay diagram that follows. Sentence *b* is placed in the diagram for you.

a. A superficial friendship is one that often makes us fall into materialistic behavior against our better judgment.

b. Nowadays, it is not easy to find good and loyal friends because there are many kinds of people with different thoughts, feelings, and even intellect.

c. Another category of friend is the selfish friend. An example of a selfish friend is someone who tries to take advantage of you.

d. Despite these differences, friendship can be classified into three categories: superficial, selfish, and real.

e. Even though we may have many kinds of friends in our lives, once we find a real one, it allows us to give the best of ourselves to make our friends feel good. I am sure this is the only kind of friendship that will be everlasting.

f. When there is a real friendship, you are always willing to share all kinds of sadness and joy with your friend.

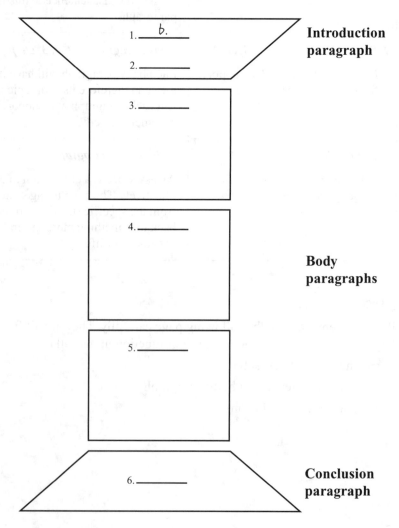

1. __b.__ **Introduction paragraph**

2. _____

3. _____ **Body paragraphs**

4. _____

5. _____

6. _____ **Conclusion paragraph**

EXERCISE 3 *Student essay on friendship*

Before reading this essay by a student from Japan, look at the questions on page 72. Then read the essay carefully, and answer the questions.

Kiyomi Kumazawa

Different Stages of Friendship

I have had experiences where I felt a closeness with a person who I had just met, and we were able to become friends instantly as if we had known each other for a long time. I can call that person a soul mate because I felt my soul drawn to him or her for no reason and irrespective of sex, age, and race. I have a friend, Kaori, who I met just once nine years ago, and I remember vividly what we did and talked about even though I don't remember her face clearly any more. However, we have kept in touch with each other to this day. An event like this happens only occasionally in our lives because it usually takes time to become friends and to cultivate friendships. For that reason, we have different kinds of friendships, depending usually on how long we have known the friends. The process of making friends can be divided into three stages: new friends and acquaintances, true friends, and best friends.

There are many reasons why people become friends such as feelings of familiarity, having things in common, or having the same experience. For example, when I was taking an English class, I had many classmates, but I could not get to know everyone. Some of them became my friends because they were friendly and easy to talk to, because we spent time doing something together in class, or because we had the same purpose: a desire to improve our English. However, some of them remained only acquaintances because we didn't keep in touch after the course without definite reasons. They were friends at that time only, and the reasons for this that come to mind are that we led busy lives and that we didn't have much in common because of no longer being classmates. However, we shared qualities of friendship such as warmth and encouraging one another at that time although we were only acquaintances.

Moving on to the second stage, a true friendship would be a deeper relationship; it is natural for us to be true friends if we spend time together and get to know one another. For instance, some of my former classmates are still my friends, and we sometimes have lunch, go shopping, or talk on the phone even though we are not classmates any more. We are becoming true friends and building friendships because we are getting to know each other better gradually on account of spending time together. As a result, we have trust, understanding, and affection in our friendships.

While cultivating a friendship, you might find a best friend whom you can confide in, whom you do all you can for without expecting anything in return, and whom you sacrifice your time or energy for willingly if he or she needs you.

continued

A best friend will accept and respect you, keep confidences, and be loyal to you. When you can get a friendship like this, it is not too much to say that you are fortunate, for it is difficult to find a best friend. That is so because it is hard to accept and respect differences in feelings, thoughts, and personalities, and also because we are afraid to reveal ourselves. Fortunately, my best friend, Mikako, and I got over these difficulties. For example, we know each other's shortcomings, and if necessary, we advise each other to mend them. However, we can accept them because we know each other very well, so they are not serious problems in our friendship. Also we confide in each other and share our personal events and feelings no matter whether they are good or bad. We want to listen to each other's opinions even if we disagree or disapprove of them because we accept and respect each other, and we know we value each other's opinions.

We have different kinds of friends in different parts of our lives, but not all friendships last forever. However, they are parts of our lives and our memories even though some of them are only acquaintances. While building a friendship, we learn and benefit from our friends through their encouragement, affection, support, trust, and kindness. When we have a good relationship with someone, it makes us feel happy and joyful. And friendship makes us more human as it helps us to realize that others have the same needs as we do that friendship fills. In the end, friendship helps us to see how precious life is and why we are living.

1. How many paragraphs does the essay have?
2. Does the introduction grab your attention? Does it move logically towards the thesis statement? What is that thesis statement?
3. Does each body paragraph have its own main idea? Is each main idea supported adequately? How are the body paragraphs related to the thesis statement?
4. Does the conclusion make you recall the thesis or think of a new idea? Would the conclusion be as effective if it were just one sentence? Explain.
5. Has Ms. Kumazawa convinced you of her thesis? Explain.

EXERCISE 4 *Topic sentence or thesis statement?*

Look at the following main idea sentences. For each one, decide whether:

a. It is a good topic sentence. It states a fairly specific idea that can be well developed in a single paragraph.

b. It is a good thesis statement. It states a more general idea that requires an essay to be developed well.

c. It could be developed into either a paragraph or an essay topic, with modifications.

Write *P* for paragraph, *E* for essay, or *P/E* for both. Be ready to defend your choices. (*Hint:* Think of how you would support these main idea sentences.)

_____ 1 Friendship and kinship are different relationships in terms of loyalty, obligation, and feeling.

_____ 2 Men and women cannot be real friends for a number of reasons.

_____ 3 We choose our friends but not our relatives: This is the basic difference between friendship and kinship.

_____ 4 There are definite qualities that I look for in a friend.

_____ 5 There are three important characteristics that all real friendships share.

_____ 6 A good friend taught me a valuable lesson about loyalty.

_____ 7 There are two kinds of friends: fair-weather friends and real friends.

_____ 8 There are several reasons for a friendship to break apart.

_____ 9 A friend becomes part of the family in my country.

_____ 10 We have different kinds of friends for different parts of our lives.

C Meeting reader expectations: Objective writing

The writing that you do in Part 2 of each chapter is personal and subjective. The assignments ask you to write about what you like and dislike, to recall similar incidents from your own life, and sometimes to write about subjects that might be too intimate for a formal audience. This expressive writing is an important step to take in developing your writing. It allows you to express informally your immediate reactions to what you read.

Later, in Part 5 of each chapter, you are asked to write more formally and objectively, to move beyond what the reading means to you personally and to express your views on issues that have meaning for others as well. At this stage, your purpose is more informative and persuasive than expressive.

In Part 5 your opinion is still important, but the reasons behind your opinion are more important and more interesting to your readers (your teacher, classmates, or some other formal audience). Your teacher will look at your composition to see how logically you present your thoughts. He or she will look at what statement you make about the topic and what proof you use to support your view. In other words, as you move from Part 2 of each chapter to Part 5, your thinking and writing will progress from the subjective to the objective.

MAKING LOGICAL ASSERTIONS

Writing objectively for a formal audience requires a slightly different approach to a topic. One way to bring objectivity to your more formal writing is to make sure that your thesis statement makes a *logical assertion*. A logical assertion is a statement of opinion or judgment that you can support with clear and valid reasons.

Which of the following statements express an opinion that can be supported logically?

1. My father is my best friend.
2. Italy won the World Cup in 1990.
3. The food in my country is the most delicious in the world.
4. There is intelligent life on other planets.
5. Computers create more employment than unemployment.

Statement 1 This may be true, but it is a subjective assertion, one that cannot be supported logically.

Statement 2 This is a matter of fact, not an opinion. Therefore, there is nothing in it that is arguable. Either it is true or it isn't.

Statement 3 This statement may also be true, but it is simply an expression of taste. There is no arguing with taste, so even a researched attempt to prove the assertion logically would have no point.

Statement 4 This may be true, but there is no way to verify it; thus, it is impossible to support logically.

Statement 5 This statement is the only logical assertion. It expresses an opinion about computers that a reader may disagree with. Logical support is necessary to convince the reader, who might easily take the opposite view without proof. Even if readers agree with the assertion, they will probably be interested in why the writer has made the assertion.

When the thesis statement of your essay is a logical assertion, your composition can be built on a firm foundation. You have a reason to think and write about the topic, and the reader has a reason to read your writing.

EXERCISE 5 *Logical assertions*

Read each statement, and decide whether it is a logical assertion that could serve as the thesis statement in an essay. If a statement is a good logical assertion, write *LA* in the blank. If you decide a statement is not a logical assertion, find the reason why in the following list of choices, and write the letter of the reason in the blank.

a. It is a subjective assertion.

b. It is not a matter of judgment or opinion; it is a matter of fact.

c. It is a question of taste.

d. It may be true, but it cannot be verified.

_____ 1 Soccer is the world's best sport.

_____ 2 Women do not drive as well as men.

_____ 3 More men than women were involved in car accidents last year.

_____ 4 Money can't buy happiness.

_____ 5 The wrong diet can lead to health problems.

_____ 6 A woman has no hope of being elected president of the United States.

_____ 7 The late John F. Kennedy would not approve of the present U.S. president's foreign policy.

_____ 8 Women and men can be friends under certain circumstances.

_____ 9 I like classical music better than popular music.

_____ 10 Friendship between people of two different cultures presents obstacles to overcome.

D Sentence grammar: Subject-verb agreement

SUBJECTS AND VERBS

Correct English sentences must have subjects and verbs that agree. Simply put, this means singular subjects should have singular verb forms, and plural subjects should have plural verb forms, as in the examples that follow. Note that the subjects are underlined and the verbs are in italics.

   a. Friendship *is* unlike other relationships.
      (A non-count noun takes a singular verb.)

   b. A friend in need *is* a friend indeed.
      (A singular noun takes a singular verb.)

   c. Most people *feel* that good friends *are* necessary to their lives.
      (Plural nouns take plural verbs.)

   d. Being able to confide in one another *is* an important component of true friendship.
      (A gerund phrase is singular, and takes a singular verb.)

   e. To be able to show your feelings *is* essential to a friendship.
      (An infinitive phrase is singular, and takes a singular verb.)

To help make subjects and verbs agree in your writing, follow the eight guidelines presented on the following pages.

Guideline 1
Subjects connected by *and* take a plural verb.

   a. Friendship and kinship *are* very different relationships.

   b. A friend and a relative *occupy* important but different places in our lives.

Guideline 2
Phrases that come between the subject and verb do not affect the verb.
(*Remember:* The subject is never part of a prepositional phrase.)

a. Friendship, unlike relations with relatives, *reflects* personal choice.
   b. Kinship, for better or worse, *is* a condition of birth that we have no choice in.

EXERCISE 6 *Subject-verb agreement: Guidelines 1 and 2*

Underline the subjects in each sentence, and circle the correct form of the verbs.

1 A friend accepts/accept our weaknesses, whereas relatives often pretends/pretend that we don't have any weaknesses.

2 Sharing confidences with friends and trusting them to be discreet is/are important requirements of friendship.

3 Loyalty, or an unspoken agreement to remain faithful and supportive, is/are more often expected in friendship than in kinship.

4 A cousin and a brother never stops/stop being relatives, but a friend sometimes does/do stop being a friend.

5 A friend, to deepen the friendly relations, shares/share his or her deepest feelings with you.

6 A relative, especially a close one, very likely knows/know how you are feeling without having to ask.

Guideline 3

The subject usually comes before the verb but can come after it. (*Remember: There* is never the subject of a sentence. It is often used in the subject position with the verb *be*. In these cases, the subject comes after the verb, and the verb agrees with it.)

   a. There *are* different categories of friend.
   b. Among the most important components of friendship *is* the ability to compromise.

Guideline 4

In relative clauses, relative pronouns *who, which,* and *that* can function as subjects. In cases like this, the verb in the clause takes its number from the word to which it refers. When a relative clause modifies a whole phrase or clause rather than a noun, its verb is singular.

   a. Friends need to see our good side, of course, but also our flaws, which *are* just as much a part of who we are.
   b. To show your bad side to others, which *includes* telling your fears, disappointments, and negative feelings, can sometimes be hard.
   c. Insightful friends can see both sides of a person, which *is* hard to do.

EXERCISE 7 *Subject-verb agreement: Guidelines 3 and 4*

Underline the subject in each sentence, and circle the correct form of each verb.

1 People who knows/know only your good side doesn't/don't know all of you.

2 Being honest about negative feelings, which includes/include saying that you have been hurt, lets/let a friend get to know you better.

3 There is/are a number of habits that can keep a friendship from growing.

4 The tendency to "keep score," which means/mean comparing what one gives to what one receives in a friendship, is a bad habit.

5 Keeping score in friendships that is/are important to you may harm the relationships.

6 Those people who has/have trouble accepting others' generosity needs/need to remember how happy they are to help a friend.

Guideline 5
When the correlative conjunctions *either . . . or* and *neither . . . nor* are used to connect two subjects, the verb agrees with the second subject.

   a. When a break in a friendship occurs, either a betrayal or <u>differing views</u> on something important *are* often the cause.

   b. When a break in a friendship occurs, either differing views on something important or a <u>betrayal</u> *is* often the cause.

When *neither* and *either* are used as quantifiers, they take singular verbs. Do not confuse them with the correlative conjunctions *either . . . or* and *neither . . . nor.*

CORRELATIVE CONJUNCTION	a. Either my sister or my <u>parents</u> *plan* to watch my house while I'm gone.
QUANTIFIER	b. <u>Neither</u> (one) of my brothers *has* the time to help me.

Guideline 6
Most indefinite pronouns, though often plural in meaning, take a singular verb. Indefinite pronouns that take a singular verb include *each, either, neither, everyone, everybody, somebody, someone, something, everything, anybody, nothing, no one,* and *nobody.*

   a. <u>Everyone</u> *needs* friends, so <u>no one</u> *is* completely happy without them.

   b. Not <u>everything</u> that *has been said* about friendship necessarily *holds* true for kinship.

Both, few, several, and *many* take plural verbs.

   c. <u>Both</u> of my brothers *have* demanding jobs.

None, some, most, and *all* take a singular verb when used with non-count nouns and a plural verb when used with plural count nouns.

d. <u>Most</u> of Tim's time *is* spent watching television.

e. <u>Most</u> of my friends *have* children.

EXERCISE 8 *Subject-verb agreement: Guidelines 5 and 6*

Underline the subjects in each sentence or clause, and circle the correct forms of the verbs.

1. An introvert is someone who is/are more interested in her or his own thoughts and feelings than in something that is/are outside herself or himself.

2. Everyone recognizes/recognize extroverts: people who likes/like to be with others and to attract attention.

3. An introvert and an extrovert both needs/need friends as everyone does/do.

4. Neither the introvert nor the extrovert is/are happy without knowing that he or she has/have friends.

5. Extroverts is/are probably better at making friends because almost everything about them is/are "friendly."

6. Neither big parties nor a very public job is/are attractive to an introvert, who prefers/prefer quieter surroundings.

7. On the other hand, either a party or another place with lots of people appeals/appeal to extroverts.

8. Most of what is/are mentioned here comes/come from research, but all of it is/are easy to observe among people that you know.

9. At some time in his or her life, every introvert probably wishes/wish to be more extroverted.

10. Truth told, no extrovert has/have been hurt by thinking quietly about life, which all of us needs/need to do at least occasionally.

Guideline 7

Group nouns (also called collective nouns) have a plural meaning but usually take a singular verb in North American English. Group nouns include *family, class, committee, government, team, audience, band, group,* and *company*.

a. My <u>family</u> *is* very large if I count all my cousins.

b. The gas <u>company</u> *employs* more people than any other company in town.

Guideline 8

Some nouns that end in *-s* appear to be plural but take singular verbs. Nouns in this category include *physics, economics, mathematics, news,* and *politics*.

a. <u>Mathematics</u> *was* my hardest subject at school.

b. No <u>news</u> *is* good news, they say.

EXERCISE 9 *Subject-verb agreement: Guidelines 7 and 8*

Underline the subject, and circle the correct form of the verb.

1 A young audience is/are often more enthusiastic than an older one.

2 He found that physics was/were more difficult for him than he had thought it would be.

3 Economics and mathematics requires/require a certain amount of concentration to understand.

4 From what they said on TV, the government is/are going to announce tax reforms soon.

5 Politics has/have never made much sense to me.

6 The news about the earthquakes was/were quite discouraging.

7 The two pieces of news John shared with us was/were both distressing.

EXERCISE 10 *Editing for subject-verb agreement*

Read the paragraph, and rewrite it to correct the subject-verb agreement errors.

   For me loyalty is an important part of friendship. A loyal friend is true and faithful to me. Loyalty to friends do not mean that my friends should support me when I am wrong, however. Sometimes people supports friends who has lied or been dishonest to others. This kind of support is not loyalty. A loyal friend would support my decision to go away to school, even if it meant our separation. A loyal friend supports decisions and actions that honestly benefits you, even if the friend lose something in the process.

Friendship

PART 5
FORMAL WRITING ASSIGNMENT

Ⓐ Writing topics

Choose an essay topic from the list below. For your formal writing assignment, you will develop an essay on the topic you choose.

1. *Comparison and contrast* Compare or contrast friendship and kinship (relationships between relatives).

2. *Cause and effect* What causes a friendship to break apart?

3. *Definition* Write your own definition of friendship.

4. Choose one of these two proverbs to write about:

    "A false friend is more dangerous than an open enemy." *(Francis Bacon, English philosopher)*

    "Friendship always benefits; love sometimes injures." *(Seneca, Roman statesman, dramatist, and philosopher)*

Ⓑ Generating ideas: Mind mapping

Drawing a mind map is a good way to generate ideas for your essay. Look at the sample mind map for topic 1 above, "Compare or contrast friendship and kinship," on the next page. Then follow these steps to create your own mind map:

1. Think of a word or phrase that characterizes how you feel about your topic and which expresses your purpose in writing. Write that word or phrase in a box in the middle of the page. (In the sample mind map for topic 1, the student has written "friendship and kinship are different.")

2. Write specific ideas on arms that lead out of the box, and on branches leading off of the arms. Draw as many arms and branches as you need. Try to get all of your ideas on paper.

3. When you finish the mind map, evaluate your ideas. Circle the ideas that you like best. Then draw lines to connect the circled ideas that go together logically.

4. Concentrating on these better ideas, write three questions that you would like to explore with classmates.

Ⓒ Expanding your point of view: Group discussion

Get together with a small group of students in your class who have chosen the same writing topic. Take turns asking the questions each of you wrote in Section B, step 4. Discuss and listen to each other's ideas.

Follow-up Quickly write down at least three new ideas that came out of your discussion.

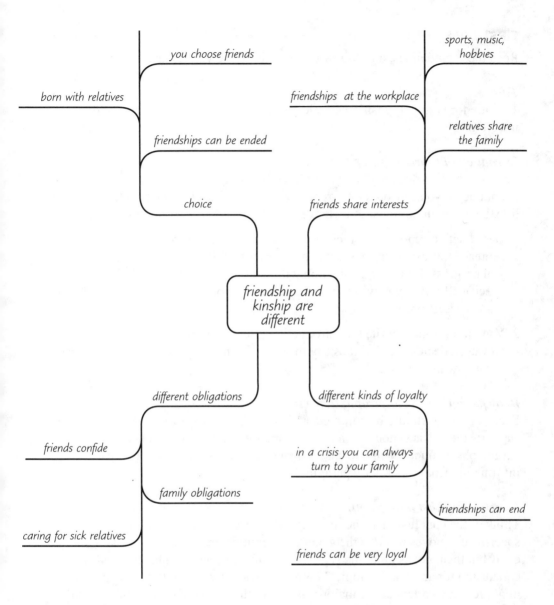

D Initial drafts

The standard academic essay has an introduction, body paragraphs, and a conclusion. In your paper, let what you have to say determine how many body paragraphs there will be.

The essay topics in this chapter are labeled by pattern of organization: comparison and contrast, cause and effect, and definition. These labels do not mean that every body paragraph must be a comparison if you chose topic 1. You can use examples and definitions to compare and contrast two ideas. Likewise, you can use a narrative to develop an essay defining friendship. The important thing to keep in mind is your *overall* purpose in writing—to compare, define, classify, or to analyze cause—and to use any patterns that serve your overall purpose.

FIRST DRAFT

Read these guidelines, and follow them as you write your essay.

Title
The title for your composition should be short, relevant to your topic, and interesting.

Introduction (Paragraph 1)
The introduction does not need to be long, but it must be more than one sentence. Do not begin your introduction by referring to the title. The introduction, not the title, begins your composition. Here are two hints about introductions:

1 Begin with a general statement about the topic; then move sentence by sentence towards your thesis statement, becoming more and more specific as you progress. End the introduction with your thesis statement, stating specifically what you will write about. Be sure your thesis statement makes a logical assertion.

2 You might want to write the introduction after you write the rest of your essay. However, decide on your thesis before writing the body to keep your purpose in mind while writing.

Body paragraphs (Paragraphs 2, 3, etc.)
Each paragraph should be complete and unified, with its own topic sentence that supports the thesis statement in the introduction. Make sure you keep body paragraphs distinct: Each one has its own main idea, so it does not repeat information from other body paragraphs.

Conclusion (Last paragraph)
Think of the conclusion as the reverse of the introduction in that it begins in the specific and moves towards the general. It reminds readers of the thesis of the essay but then moves on to the significance of your ideas in a bigger context. A conclusion for an essay on topic 2 (What causes a friendship to break apart?) might remind readers of the major reasons for the break up of a friendship and then mention that these are reasons we all need to pay attention to because we all need friends.

REVISION

Before revising, study the criteria listed in the *Essay Assessment Checklist* on page 84. Revise your first draft with these criteria in mind. Label this new draft "Draft 2."

E Review, revision, and assessment

PEER FEEDBACK

Read a classmate's paper and give feedback using the *Essay Assessment Checklist* on page 84. Write your comments on the checklist, but make no marks on your classmate's paper. Give the checklist and the paper back to the writer. Answer any questions your classmate has about your feedback.

FURTHER REVISION

What did you learn from the feedback you received? Is your essay successful—is it convincing, interesting, clearly organized, and complete? If not, how can you make it more successful?

Revise your paper using the feedback you got from your classmates. Give your teacher all drafts (with the last draft marked "Final draft") and the *Essay Assessment Checklist* completed by your classmate.

Writer's name: _____

Reader's name: _____

Essay Assessment Checklist   Chapter 3

These are the criteria for a well-written essay. Use them to examine your writing, or a classmate's, and check *Yes* or *No* for each item. You may wish to add comments or suggestions.

Content and ideas

	Yes	No	Reader's comments
1 The writer has thought carefully about the topic and has a clear thesis.	❑	❑	
2 The writer supports the main points enough to give the reader a reason to believe them.	❑	❑	
3 The writer's voice is clear because he or she writes in a sincere way and keeps the audience in mind.	❑	❑	
4 The reader wants to continue reading to the end. It's interesting.	❑	❑	

Organization and form

	Yes	No	Reader's comments
5 The essay has a clear beginning, middle, and end. There is a title at the top, with separate introductory, body, and concluding paragraphs.	❑	❑	
6 The essay moves logically in a straight line. The reader can understand the thesis and other main points fully after one reading.	❑	❑	

Language

	Yes	No	Reader's comments
7 The paper is easy to understand. These elements are used well:			
• sentence structure (no fragments or run-on sentences)	❑	❑	
• grammar (subject-verb agreement)	❑	❑	
• vocabulary	❑	❑	
• mechanics (spelling, capitalization, punctuation)	❑	❑	

CHAPTER 4

Live to Work or Work to Live?

- Where might the ant be going with the kernel of corn?
- What do its actions suggest about its attitude toward work?

PART 1

INTRODUCTION TO THE TOPIC, READING, AND DISCUSSION

A Reflection

Aesop, who is believed to have lived in ancient Greece, was the author of many fables. A fable is a very short story told to teach a lesson, or moral. Read Aesop's fable. Then discuss the following question with a classmate:

Are you more like the ant or the grasshopper in this story?

The Ant and the Grasshopper

An Aesop Fable

A grasshopper was singing away one summer's day when an ant came plodding* by, bent under the weight of a kernel of corn.

"Why work so hard in this fine warm weather?" the grasshopper called to the ant. "Why not enjoy yourself, like me?"

"I'm storing up food for the winter," the ant replied. "And I suggest you do the same." 5

"Winter!" scoffed* the grasshopper. "Who cares about winter! We have more food than we can eat."

The ant held his tongue and went about his business.

Then winter set in, and soon the grasshopper couldn't find so much as a grain 10 of barley or wheat. He went to the ant to beg for some food, knowing the ant had plenty.

"Friend grasshopper," said the ant, "you sang while I slaved away* last summer, and laughed at me besides. Sing now and see what it will get you."

Moral: *Save for the future and you won't be without.* 15

---

plodding: *moving along slowly without resting*
scoffed: *laughed, mocked*
slaved away: *worked hard*

B Discussion

Discuss these questions in pairs, in small groups, or as a class.

1 During the summer months, which insect seems more content?

2 How does the situation change in the winter?

3 Do you think most people live according to the moral of the fable? Do you live that way?

4 In the lives of real people, is industry (hard work) usually rewarded and idleness punished?

C Preparing to read

NOTES ON THE READING

This reading by W. Somerset Maugham, also called "The Ant and the Grasshopper," is a humorous variation on Aesop's fable and is based on a version of the fable written by Jean La Fontaine. Maugham tells the story of the industrious George Ramsay. To help us understand the present situation in the story, the author gives us background information about the past. We learn about George's younger brother, Tom, who has always been the black sheep in the family. Tom is the one who is different from other family members, less respectable, and a source of worry to George. But Tom has a lot of charm, which is the ability to please, fascinate, or attract other people. George resembles the ant, and Tom resembles the grasshopper in the fable.

Work with a partner. With what you have learned about George and Tom from the notes, guess whether the following words and phrases describe George or Tom. Write *G* for George or *T* for Tom.

_____ 1 **philander** (to have sexual relationships outside one's marriage)

_____ 2 a life of industry and **thrift** (spending money carefully)

_____ 3 **promises of amendment** (promises to change one's behavior)

_____ 4 **idle** (lazy, avoiding work)

_____ 5 a small income from **gilt-edged securities** (safe investments)

_____ 6 **blackmail** (threaten to act a certain way unless you are paid money)

_____ 7 **end in the gutter** (end up poor, living in the street)

PREVIEWING THE VOCABULARY

Before reading, preview the vocabulary in context. Read these key sentences based on the text, and choose the best meaning for the underlined words.

1 The fable "The Ant and the Grasshopper" is devised to bring home to the young the useful lesson that, in an imperfect world, industry is rewarded and giddiness punished.

   a. hard work

   b. seriousness

   c. lack of seriousness

2. Winter comes and the ant is comfortably provided for, but the grasshopper has an empty <u>larder</u>.

   a. wallet

   b. place where food is kept

   c. underground nest where ants live

3. I never saw anyone wear an expression of such deep <u>gloom</u>. I was sorry for him. "How are you?" I asked. "I'm not <u>in hilarious spirits</u>," he said.

   a. hopelessness / very happy

   b. happiness / in a good mood

   c. hopelessness / in a bad mood

4. "Why don't you <u>chuck</u> him? You've done everything in the world for him. You must know by now that he's quite hopeless."

   a. talk to

   b. leave to himself; discard

   c. encourage to live a better life

5. I suppose every family has a black sheep. Tom had been <u>a sore trial</u> to his family for twenty years.

   a. a source of pride

   b. a source of amusement

   c. a problem; an annoyance

6. But one day, without warning, Tom announced that he didn't like work and that he <u>wasn't suited for</u> marriage. He wanted to enjoy himself. He would listen to no <u>expostulations</u>.

   a. wasn't ready for / relatives

   b. didn't like / members of his wife's family

   c. didn't have the right qualities for / arguments to change his mind

7. George asked Tom what would happen when his money was spent. They soon found out: he borrowed. He was charming but <u>unscrupulous</u>.

   a. dishonest

   b. courteous

   c. full of principles

8. Tom did not waste his charm on George. George was a serious man and <u>insensible to such enticements</u>.

   a. could not resist his brother's charm

   b. not persuaded by his brother's charm

   c. always ready to help his brother with money

9 When circumstances forced George to realize that his brother would never settle down and he washed his hands of him, Tom, without <u>a qualm</u>, began to blackmail him.

   a. a penny

   b. a reason

   c. hesitation

10 Tom had high spirits, and unfailing gaiety, and incredible charm. I never <u>grudged</u> the contributions he regularly <u>levied on me</u> for the necessities of his existence.

   a. liked / asked me for

   b. hated / stole from me

   c. was unwilling to give him / collected (like a tax)

11 Poor George! I sympathized with him. I wondered now as I sat down beside him what <u>infamous</u> thing Tom had done.

   a. interesting

   b. terrible, shameful

   c. surprising, unexpected

12 'And you can't deny that Tom has been an idle, worthless, dissolute, and dishonourable <u>rogue</u>. If there were any justice, he'd be in the workhouse.'

   a. unlucky man

   b. man without principles

   c. man with high principles

13 George Ramsay beat his clenched fist on the table. 'It's not fair, I tell you, it's not fair. Damn it, it's not fair.' I could not help it. I burst into a shout of laughter as I looked at George's <u>wrathful</u> face.

   a. angry

   b. happy

   c. humorous

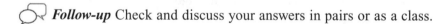 *Follow-up* Check and discuss your answers in pairs or as a class.

LANGUAGE NOTES

British spelling is used in this story. In addition, some words and expressions are typically British, and a few are very out-of-date.

British Spelling	American Spelling
learnt	learned
apologise	apologize
favourite	favorite
honourable	honorable
rumours	rumors

Saving your presence, ... (line 12): Without meaning to annoy you, ...
as if he had just stepped out of a bandbox (line 57): very well dressed
scapegrace (line 65): rascal; habitually unscrupulous character
fortnight (line 66): two weeks time
Providence (line 90): God's care
workhouse (line 93): home for poor people
sovereign (line 105): an old British gold coin

D Reading for overall meaning

Read the story at a quick but comfortable pace. As you read, think about this question:

Do you think the message in Maugham's story is the same as or different from the message in the Aesop fable of the ant and the grasshopper?

The Ant and the Grasshopper

W. Somerset Maugham

When I was a very small boy I was made to learn by heart certain of the fables of La Fontaine, and the moral of each was carefully explained to me. Among those I learnt was *The Ant and the Grasshopper,* which is devised to bring home to the young the useful lesson that in an imperfect world industry is rewarded and giddiness punished. In this admirable fable (I apologise for telling something which everyone is politely, but inexactly, supposed to know) the ant spends a laborious summer gathering its winter store, while the grasshopper sits on a blade of grass singing to the sun. Winter comes and the ant is comfortably provided for, but the grasshopper has an empty larder: he goes to the ant and begs for a little food. Then the ant gives him her classic answer:
  'What were you doing in the summer time?'
  'Saving your presence, I sang, I sang all day, all night.'
  'You sang. Why, then go and dance.'
  I could not help thinking of this fable when the other day I saw George Ramsay lunching by himself in a restaurant. I never saw anyone wear an expression of such deep gloom. He was staring into space. He looked as though the burden of the whole world sat on his shoulders. I was sorry for him: I suspected at once that his unfortunate brother had been causing trouble again. I went up to him and held out my hand.
  'How are you?' I asked.
  'I'm not in hilarious spirits,' he answered.
  'Is it Tom again?'
  He sighed.
  'Yes, it's Tom again.'

continued

'Why don't you chuck him? You've done everything in the world for him. You must know by now that he's quite hopeless.'

I suppose every family has a black sheep. Tom had been a sore trial to his for twenty years. He had begun life decently enough: he went into business, married, and had two children. The Ramsays were perfectly respectable people and there was every reason to suppose that Tom Ramsay would have a useful and honourable career. But one day, without warning, he announced that he didn't like work and that he wasn't suited for marriage. He wanted to enjoy himself. He would listen to no expostulations. He left his wife and his office. He had a little money and he spent two happy years in the various capitals of Europe. Rumours of his doings reached his relations from time to time and they were profoundly shocked. He certainly had a very good time. They shook their heads and asked what would happen when his money was spent. They soon found out: he borrowed. He was charming and unscrupulous. I have never met anyone to whom it was more difficult to refuse a loan. He made a steady income from his friends and he made friends easily. But he always said that the money you spent on necessities was boring; the money that was amusing to spend was the money you spent on luxuries. For this he depended on his brother George. He did not waste his charm on him. George was a serious man and insensible to such enticements. George was respectable. Once or twice he fell to Tom's promises of amendment and gave him considerable sums in order that he might make a fresh start. On these Tom bought a motor-car and some very nice jewelry. But when circumstances forced George to realize that his brother would never settle down and he washed his hands of him, Tom, without a qualm, began to blackmail him. It was not very nice for a respectable lawyer to find his brother shaking cocktails behind the bar of his favourite restaurant or to see him waiting on the boxseat of a taxi outside his club. Tom said that to serve in a bar or to drive a taxi was a perfectly decent occupation, but if George could oblige him with a couple of hundred pounds he didn't mind for the honour of the family giving it up. George paid.

For twenty years Tom raced and gambled, philandered with the prettiest girls, danced, ate in the most expensive restaurants, and dressed beautifully. He always looked as if he had just stepped out of a bandbox. Though he was forty-six you would never have taken him for more than thirty-five. He was a most amusing companion, and though you knew he was perfectly worthless you could not but enjoy his society. He had high spirits and unfailing gaiety and incredible charm. I never grudged the contributions he regularly levied on me for the necessities of his existence. I never lent him fifty pounds without feeling that I was in his debt. Tom Ramsay knew everyone and everyone knew Tom Ramsay. You could not approve of him, but you could not help liking him.

Poor George, only a year older than his scapegrace brother, looked sixty. He had never taken more than a fortnight's holiday in the year for a quarter of a century. He was in his office every morning at nine-thirty and never left it till six. He was honest, industrious, and worthy. He had a good wife, to whom he

continued

had never been unfaithful even in thought, and four daughters to whom he was the best of fathers. He made a point of saving a third of his income and his plan was to retire at fifty-five to a little house in the country where he proposed to cultivate his garden and play golf. His life was blameless. He was glad that he was growing old because Tom was growing old too. He rubbed his hands and said:

'It was all very well when Tom was young and good-looking, but he's only a year younger than I am. In four years he'll be fifty. He won't find life so easy then. I shall have thirty thousand pounds by the time I'm fifty. For twenty-five years I've said that Tom would end in the gutter. And we shall see how he likes that. We shall see if it really pays best to work or be idle.'

Poor George! I sympathized with him. I wondered now as I sat down beside him what infamous thing Tom had done. George was evidently very much upset.

'Do you know what's happened now?' he asked me.

I was prepared for the worst. I wondered if Tom had got into the hands of the police at last. George could hardly bring himself to speak.

'You're not going to deny that all my life I've been hardworking, decent, respectable, and straightforward. After a life of industry and thrift I can look forward to retiring on a small income in gilt-edged securities. I've always done my duty in that state of life in which it has pleased Providence to place me.'

'True.'

'And you can't deny that Tom has been an idle, worthless, dissolute, and dishonourable rogue. If there were any justice he'd be in the workhouse.'

'True.'

George grew red in the face.

'A few weeks ago he became engaged to a woman old enough to be his mother. And now she's died and left him everything she had. Half a million pounds, a yacht, a house in London, and a house in the country.'

George Ramsay beat his clenched fist on the table.

'It's not fair, I tell you, it's not fair. Damn it, it's not fair.'

I could not help it. I burst into a shout of laughter as I looked at George's wrathful face, I rolled in my chair, I very nearly fell on the floor. George never forgave me. But Tom often asks me to excellent dinners in his charming house in Mayfair, and if he occasionally borrows a trifle from me, that is merely from force of habit. It is never more than a sovereign.

 Follow-up Now answer this question:

> Do you think the message in Maugham's story is the same as or different from the message in the Aesop's fable of the ant and the grasshopper?

E Reading for more detail

Read the story a second time. Use the questions to read for more detail and to bring your experience to the reading.

1. What things didn't George Ramsay like about his brother Tom? Do you feel the same way about Tom?

2. How was it that Tom always had money if he didn't work regularly? Why did George give Tom money even after George had "washed his hands of him"?

3. Why was George so upset by Tom's good fortune at the end of the story? Were you happy for Tom or upset like George?

4. Considering the narrator's reaction at the end of the story, what do you think his opinion of Tom is?

5. How is the message in Maugham's story different from the message in the fable?

6. *Key words* Make a list of six words or expressions that you feel are important to the story. Be ready to explain what each word means and why it is important.

Follow-up Discuss your answers in pairs, in small groups, or as a class.

PART 2
PERSONAL WRITTEN RESPONSE

Ⓐ Journals: A private audience

Choose two of the following topics. Write for about 20 minutes in your journal notebook. Express yourself honestly. These journal entries are for your eyes only, so do not spend a lot of time using a dictionary or worrying about grammar.

1. Which insect from the fable, the ant or the grasshopper, do you resemble more in personality? How?
2. Which of the two brothers in the story do you admire more? Why?
3. Does either Tom or George remind you of someone you know? Who? In what ways?

Ⓑ Shared writing

Choose two of the following topics, and write for a total of 20 minutes. Your audience is your classmates, with whom you will share your writing. They will be interested not only in what you feel but also in why you feel that way. Express your views clearly and support them.

1. Which moral, or message, do you agree with, the one in the Aesop's fable or the one in Maugham's story? Why?
2. Write a letter to Tom or George, giving him advice on how to improve his life. Explain the reasons for the advice you give.
3. Which "The Ant and the Grasshopper" is closer to real life, Aesop's fable or the Maugham story? Why?

Ⓒ Feedback on your writing

Get feedback on how clear and logical your thinking and writing are. Select one of the questions from *Shared Writing,* and read your answer to a small group of classmates. Follow the *Peer Feedback Guidelines* on page 11.

PART 3

FURTHER READING, WRITING, AND DISCUSSION

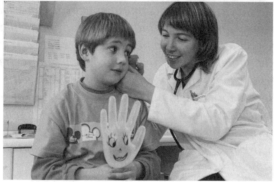

- Many women work and are very good mothers. What determines their success as mothers?
- Are women who stay at home necessarily better mothers?

A Preparing to read

NOTES ON THE READING

Redbook magazine published an article about working mothers and stay-at-home mothers and their decisions to work or not. In this selection you will read letters sent to the magazine in response to that article. The letters are from women of different social backgrounds, and two letters are from children. The title of the article, "Mommy Wars, Part II," indicates how seriously women take the issue of whether to work or to stay home and take care of their children. For some, the decision is easy. Others mention the difficulty of achieving a *balance* between work and family, that is, of being able to do both—successfully. Others have *conflicted feelings:* they want to work, and they want to stay home and take care of their children. A short introduction from the editors of the magazine precedes the letters from the readers. The letters the editors received told them they had *hit a nerve*. In other words, the magazine had touched on an issue that women are very sensitive about.

(*Note:* Words in italics are from the reading.)

B Reading for overall meaning

Read the letters for the first time to answer these questions:

Which letter and opinion do you sympathize with most? Which letter irritates, or bothers, you, if any?

Mommy Wars, Part II

Hundreds of you deluged us with fiery tomes about our April roundtable on stay-at-home vs. working moms, so we knew we'd hit a nerve. Here, we let you sound off.

Some of us work because we have to, some of us work because we want to—and some of us move heaven and earth to find a way to stay home with our kids. But no matter what we decide, achieving a perfect balance between work and family is far from easy. How much can we give to our jobs without cheating our children—and vice versa? How can we balance our own needs with everyone else's? Can we really do it all? Your letters make it clear that none of you makes these decisions quickly or lightly—and that even once you've chosen your direction, you may have strong, often conflicted feelings about it. The one resounding truth: Balancing work and family is the most difficult and divisive personal issue of our generation, and it creates tension on both sides.

The Case for Staying at Home

I made my decision to be a stay-at-home mom based on the years I worked in a day-care facility. I realized that it was impossible to satisfy the needs of small children who really just wanted to be with their mothers. The longer I worked there, the more convinced I became that I never wanted my child to be without me, so when my son was born, I stayed home to raise him.

—*Jamie G., Elgin, IL*

At Home, With Doubts

I've always said that staying home with my two sons was the best thing I've ever done for my children but the worst thing I did for myself. My career is now totally off-track because I've been home for 13 years. One of my sons recently

continued

said that I'm around too much—this is the same little boy who would cry if I even mentioned going back to work. Would I do it all over again? I really don't know.

—*Josee D., Parksville, British Columbia*

Working Moms Fight Back

In this article several of the stay-at-home moms claimed that the working moms were selfish, unloving, and didn't spend enough time having fun with their children. Being a working mother myself, I can tell you that this couldn't be further from the truth. There are just as many "good mothers" who work as there are "good mothers" who stay home. It's unfair to assess a mother's love, parenting skills, and concern for her child's well-being by whether or not she works.

—*Lori E., Shirley, IN*

I'm an attentive, nurturing, and caring mother to two sons, and I also have a job. I realize that what stay-at-home moms do every day isn't a piece of cake. However, if I respect what they do, why can't they respect what I do? The bottom line is that everyone has to do what is right for her family, and those choices should be accepted and respected.

—*Name withheld*

Yet Some of Us Have to Work

I'm a working mom, not to make me happy, but to give my children a more enjoyable life. Without my salary, we wouldn't be able to afford our nice house or have money to put away for college. I have nothing against stay-at-home moms; in fact, I actually envy them. If I ever hit the lottery, I'd quit my job in a minute.

—*Hawley G., Camp Hill, PA*

What Your Kids Have to Say

I want to give working moms a few words of encouragement. I'm a high-school student with a working mother, and I'm happy that she works. My mom is a single parent and has always had to work. Being a working mother doesn't mean that you don't love your kid—I know my mom loves me more than anything and that she's doing this because she wants me to have a good life.

—*Jade R., Holland, MI*

As a 12-year-old with a working mom, I couldn't believe that 20 percent of the stay-at-home moms in your poll think that moms like mine are selfish! As my mother said, "It's not about being selfish, it's about survival."

—*Krista B., Lyle, MN*

continued

Seeing Both Sides

A woman can be a good mother whether she carries around a laptop or a diaper bag! What makes the woman happiest is what's most important—if she's not happy staying at home, then how can she bring up a healthy, happy child?
—*Lisa J., Brampton, Ontario*

I'm a stay-at-home mom with two young children. I'm also a college graduate with only one year of work experience. Does the fact that I stay home automatically make me a perfect mother with perfect children? Am I a less interesting person and a failure at female independence because I don't work? Absolutely not on both counts! There just isn't a simple formula for the perfect mother.
—*Michelle S., Sparks, NV*

Some Have Even Found Balance

I'm a working mother and make no apologies for it because I choose to work. I stayed home for seven years, and I won't pretend it was always wonderful. I wanted to be more than my husband's wife and my children's mother—I needed my own identity. In going back to work, I've found a new level of confidence, and I have yet to see a real difference in the kids whose mothers stay at home or go to work.
—*Jeanette W., Warwick Township, PA*

 Follow-up Now answer these questions:

> Which letter and opinion do you sympathize with most? Which letter irritates, or bothers, you, if any?

ⓒ Reading for more detail

Read the selection again. Mark any places in the text that are still unclear to you.

ⓓ Helping each other understand

Write for about 20 minutes on this selection. Write about one or more of the questions below.

1. What do you have trouble understanding?
2. What was your reaction to this selection? Do you feel strongly about the topic? Why?
3. Do you think women and children from other parts of the world would make the same comments or different ones?

> *Follow-up* To a small group of students, read what you have written. Read your reaction a second time if necessary. Each group member will respond with (1) a question, (2) a comment, and/or (3) help with what you didn't understand.

E Discussion: Critical thinking

Discuss these questions in pairs, in small groups, or as a class.

1 Why does society give more responsibility for raising children to mothers than to fathers?

2 In Maugham's story, George and Tom obviously don't get along well. Do their different attitudes toward work explain why they don't get along? Is there another possible explanation?

3 The writer of the last letter, "Some Have Even Found Balance," wrote that she felt more "balanced" when she worked. Is it important for a person to work in order to feel balanced and be a complete person?

4 In a family where the mother is more employable than the husband, does it make more sense for him to be a househusband and for her to be a working mother? Explain.

PART 4
FOCUS ON WRITING SKILLS

Ⓐ Using another's writing: Summarizing a story

The process of summarizing another's writing helps you to better understand what the author is saying, as well as develop your own writing skills. When writing an essay, summarizing enables you to refer to a long story like Maugham's in a briefer form.

EXERCISE 1 *Summary of "The Ant and the Grasshopper"*
Write a summary of Maugham's story, "The Ant and the Grasshopper," in 85 words or less. Start by stating the moral, or message, of the story. Then briefly tell what happened in the story, keeping the message of the story in mind and telling it in your own words. Begin with these words to give the author's moral, or message:

In "The Ant and the Grasshopper," Maugham tells us . . .

> *Follow-up* Exchange summaries with another student. Discuss the similarities and differences in your summaries.

Ⓑ Meeting reader expectations: Introductions and conclusions

For the essay you will write in Part 5 of this chapter, your teacher will expect you to include a well-written introduction and conclusion. Look again at how Maugham introduced and concluded his story (lines 1–13 and 101–105). Then answer the questions below.

1. Does the introduction catch your interest and make you want to read further?
2. Does it give you an idea of what the story will be about?
3. Does the conclusion let you know what the writer thinks of what has happened? Would the writer's message be complete without this particular conclusion?
4. How long are the introduction and conclusion in relation to the whole story?
5. How is the introduction organized—from the general to the specific or from the specific to the general?

INTRODUCTIONS

There are many ways to introduce an essay. Just as Maugham used a fable in his story, sometimes writers use:

- an anecdote (a very short story)
- a quotation

- a question
- background necessary for the reader to understand their point

It is helpful to think of the introduction as progressing from the general to the specific. This means that you introduce the topic in a general way, as Maugham did. Then you move logically toward your thesis statement, a more specific statement about the topic at the end of the introduction.

CONCLUSIONS

Conclusions are as varied as introductions. Conclusions leave the reader with some final thoughts (but not new ideas) on the main idea and the supporting points. In a conclusion writers can:

- explain the significance of their points to their own life
- discuss how the reader might use their information
- briefly list the main points of support again for the readers to keep in mind, especially in a very long composition

Conclusions, like introductions, are typically more general than body paragraphs because they move away from the specific topic and shift toward the reader's or the writer's life. The flow in a typical essay is from *general* (the beginning) to *specific* (the thesis statement and body) and back to *general* (the conclusion). Visually, the form of an essay might look like this:

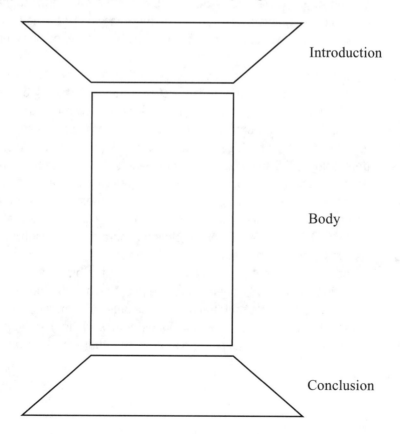

EXERCISE 2 *Student essay*

Before reading this essay by a student from Azerbaijan, preview the questions at the end of the essay on page 104. As you read the essay, notice that the writer uses examples from his own reading to support his ideas, not just the selections in this chapter.

Igor Shchegolev

Work and Labor

There are many opinions about the question, "Why don't people work?" Aesop's famous fable clearly illustrates what the result of not working is. The ant and grasshopper are opposites in that one of them doesn't want to work. People of many generations have accepted the moral of Aesop's fable as the rule. According to Aesop's moral, the ant was right, and the grasshopper was not because it did not work during the summer. It was singing and dancing all the time and didn't anticipate what would happen in the winter. That is a simple moral. It is also too idealistic. For Aesop, the world is divided into two groups—the ants and the grasshoppers. However, people in real life are more varied and complex than the ant and the grasshopper. Maugham tried to depict the world in more realistic colors. He showed two brothers, one of whom didn't work but was still rewarded. It is the way life is. So, Aesop defined a rule and Maugham showed that people don't always want to live by the rules. Why? Life is more complicated than an Aesop's fable because there is a big difference between labor and work.

Most people consider labor as a way to exist, to provide themselves with the necessities of life. They work in order to live—even if they hate their jobs—and they would not work if they could manage not to. A work ethic and moral rules have been created by society. Political orientation does not matter; in any case, society will create conditions that require people to work hard. In "The Work Ethic Is Underemployed," Daniel Yankelovich considers three conceptions of work: first, as labor, as a way to exist; second, as a way to improve one's level of life; and third, as a moral necessity. Some people accept these rules. They work hard and consider this way of living as the only right one. They believe that their labor will eventually be rewarded. They are obvious characters of Aesop's fable. They are ants. And they do labor, not work.

There is another reason that people work. It doesn't fit into any of Yankelovich's definitions of work. There are some people who work not for money, not for the best possible material life, not because of a moral necessity or society's rules—but because they cannot live without working. For them, work is a natural necessity that has nothing to do with either morals or money.

continued

There are three good examples of people who illustrate that work is different from labor. A good example of someone who could not live without working was Wolfgang Amadeus Mozart, the great Viennese musician and composer. He could not accept life without making music. To live without creating music was meaningless to him. Jack London, a great American writer, spent his entire life in an effort to describe people with strong personalities and willpower, people who were trying to realize the truth about life. Roald Amundsen, the great Norwegian explorer, sacrificed his life for the work of exploration. He was the first person to reach the South Pole.

The people I have been talking about lived in order to work. They considered work something very interesting. It made existence more exciting; it gave meaning to their lives. Life and work were the same for them. However, they don't fit into the characters of Aesop's ant or Yankelovich's workers. The three of them spent long periods of time without working. These were times of terrible depression, stress, and even the threat of madness. Mozart was under a depression after his mother's death. The last years of his life, he drank heavily, and he died in poverty. Jack London wasn't more successful: alcoholism and financial problems led him to commit suicide at the age of 40. Roald Amundsen was killed during the air search for an Italian explorer, Umberto Nobile. It would be very simple to say that these people didn't do any real work because they were lazy or because they could not handle problems due to a weak will. However, like a glowworm, which does nothing at all, they made a beautiful light through their work. The light they made illuminated whole generations.

I believe that the difference between work and labor can explain a lot of things. Sometimes it is difficult to recognize the difference between them, but it is important to do so. Since earliest times humans have created. Their creativity has brought the greatest advances and inventions into the world. Uncreative work, or labor, leaves no trace in history. The majestic pyramids of Egypt, built through the labor of thousands of slaves but the work of only a few architects, still stand today as a monument to creative work. They are a combination of work and labor. So, why are we trying to differentiate the two terms? First, it is important to understand the difference between work and labor. Second, it is important to work rather than labor in order to create rather than merely produce.

Work Cited

Yankelovich, Daniel. "The Work Ethic is Underemployed." *Psychology Today* (May 1982): 5, 6, 8.

Answer the questions.

1. Which of the four ways to introduce an essay did Mr. Shchegolev use?
2. Did you want to continue reading after you finished the introduction?
3. What is the writer's thesis? Does it appear in a thesis statement? If so, underline it.
4. How effectively does Mr. Shchegolev develop his thesis? How does he explain the difference between *work* and *labor*?
5. Mr. Shchegolev uses the ideas of a respected writer, Daniel Yankelovich, to explain three different reasons for working. What are the three reasons? Is this support effective?
6. Which of the three ways to conclude an essay presented on page 101 did Mr. Shchegolev use? Is his conclusion effective?
7. How long are the introduction and conclusion in relation to the body of the essay? The right length? Too long? Too short?
8. How closely does the form of the composition follow the general-to-specific-to-general diagram in the previous section?

Follow-up Compare and discuss your answers in pairs, in small groups, or as a class.

C Sentence grammar: Adding coherence

COHESIVE DEVICES

Writing is said to have *coherence* when the relationships between events and ideas are presented in a clear, logical way. When writing has coherence, it is easy to follow. By making the connections between your ideas clear, you help the reader stay on track and understand your message more easily.

Read this paragraph, which has little coherence and is therefore hard to understand.

Paragraph A

There were only 10 minutes left in the class. The teacher rushed to put all the rules and examples on the board. The students took out their notebooks to copy the rules down. They were a little upset. The students had an assignment with the present perfect tense. They weren't sure they would be able to do the assignment correctly. They didn't have enough oral practice with the present perfect tense.

Although the language is perfect and the sentences are short and simple, this paragraph is challenging for a reader because it lacks coherence. Each action is clear in itself, but the relationship between the different sentences is not clear.

Now read the revised paragraph. This paragraph is easier to understand because of the addition of *cohesive devices,* or words and phrases that make the relationships between the events clear to the reader. As you read the paragraph, see if you can identify some of the cohesive devices.

Paragraph B
(1)There were only 10 minutes left in the class, so the teacher rushed to put all the rules and examples for the present perfect tense on the board. (2)The students took out their notebooks to copy the rules down. (3)However, the students were a little upset because they had an assignment with the present perfect for the next day, and they weren't sure they would be able to do it correctly. (4)In addition, they were upset because they hadn't had enough oral practice with the present perfect.

Read the list of cohesive devices below, and look at examples of them in Paragraph B.

1 *Pronouns*
Pronouns (*it, they, his, her,* etc.) add coherency by referring back to a noun that has already been mentioned. For example, in sentence 3, the pronoun *it* in sentence 3, which refers to the assignment mentioned in the first part of the sentence.

2 *Coordinating conjunctions*
Coordinating conjunctions (*and, so, but,* etc.) help clarify the relationship between the two ideas they connect. In sentence 1 the coordinating conjunction *so* helps the reader understand that the first event (having only a short time left) led to the second event (the teacher rushing).

3 *Subordinating conjunctions*
Subordinating conjunctions (*because, if, when, although,* etc.) explain the relationship between the two clauses that they join. For example, in sentence 3, *because* explains the relationship between the two clauses. That is, it explains why the students were upset, which was not made clear in paragraph A.

4 *Transition words*
Transition words (*however, in addition,* etc.) make clear how a sentence relates to the previous sentence. In sentence 4, *in addition* introduces another reason why the students were upset.

5 *Repetition of an important word*
Repetition of a word reinforces the connection between the ideas in two sentences. See the use of *upset* in sentences 3 and 4.

6 *Verb tenses*
Verb tenses help show the relationship in time between events. The use of past perfect in sentence 4 helps the reader see that not practicing enough caused the students to be upset.

EXERCISE 3 *Adding coherence to a paragraph*

Read the paragraph. Then choose the best cohesive device for each numbered position. Finally, rewrite the paragraph, inserting your choices and making any necessary changes in capitalization and punctuation.

    A researcher helps explain a problem that many workers complain of. Most workers want to do their best. (1)They do not work as hard as they could. (2)They feel that others receive the benefits of their hard work. (3)The researcher doesn't see this attitude as a sign of a weak work ethic. (4)He feels the attitude would change if workers made more of the decisions that affect their work. There is a message for managers in this research. Managers need to allow workers to express their needs. (5)They need to listen to what workers say.

1. a. However,
    b. For example,
    c. Therefore,
2. a. even though
    b. because
    c. whereas
3. a. First,
    b. Unfortunately,
    c. (no cohesive device needed)
4. a. Rather,
    b. In addition,
    c. (no cohesive device needed)
5. a. or
    b. but
    c. and

EXERCISE 4 *More practice adding coherence to paragraphs*

Read the paragraph which follows. Then choose the best cohesive device for each numbered position. Finally, rewrite the paragraph, inserting your choices and making any necessary changes in capitalization and punctuation.

Some companies do actually try to address their workers' needs and suggestions. ⁽¹⁾A few companies offer day-care facilities for workers' children. ⁽²⁾Workers can have more contact with their children during the day. The workers' minds are freed from worries about their children. ⁽³⁾Theoretically, they work better. ⁽⁴⁾Some other companies offer their employees flexible working hours. Workers can begin and finish work at times they choose. ⁽⁵⁾They still have to put in the required number of hours. ⁽⁶⁾If they begin work late, they have to stay late. Other companies are listening to workers' suggestions about improving efficiency in the factory or office. ⁽⁷⁾Managers still make the final decisions, they have begun to consider the workers' input when making those decisions.

1 a. On the whole,
   b. For instance,
   c. At the beginning,
2 a. On the contrary,
   b. (no cohesive device needed)
   c. That way,
3 a. and, for example,
   b. , so
   c. however,
4 a. (no cohesive device needed)
   b. For example,
   c. Finally,
5 a. because
   b. Besides,
   c. Of course,
6 a. Therefore,
   b. However,
   c. Moreover,
7 a. Since
   b. Even though
   c. Precisely because

EXERCISE 5 *Editing for coherence*

Edit this paragraph for coherence. Read it carefully, and insert cohesive devices where they are needed. Then rewrite the paragraph.

English, like other languages, has conflicting sayings about important matters like love, friendship, and work. In English we say about work, "Never put off till tomorrow what you can do today." The message is that one can and should always work more—at least until all the work is done. In English we have this proverb: "All work and no play makes Jack a dull boy." The advice is not to work too much. Life without recreation makes one an uninteresting person. How is it that the language has two sayings that give opposite messages? We can assume that work is important to native English speakers. They respect it a lot—perhaps too much. The second saying may be a kind of safety valve. It warns people against going too far in following the advice of the first saying.

PART 5
FORMAL WRITING ASSIGNMENT

A Writing topics

Read the following essay topics, and choose the one that interests you the most.

1. *Cause and effect* Why do people work? Think about the readings and your own knowledge of human nature. (*Note:* If you feel people work only for money, it would be wise to choose another topic.)

2. *Comparison and contrast* What different qualities do men and women bring to the workplace? Do men have some good qualities that women lack, and vice versa?

3. How can we solve the conflict of working mothers? In other words, what should society do to help women balance work and family if they must or want to work?

4. *Description* What makes a good worker? If you were a manager, how would you like your workers to be?

5. Does your language have a fable like "The Ant and the Grasshopper," a fable that encourages people to work hard? How does your culture look at the division of work and recreation?

B Generating ideas: Looping

Looping is a way of freewriting in which you identify and write about new main ideas that arise as you write.

Follow these steps to use looping to generate ideas.

1. With your topic in mind, write freely for five minutes. Write without stopping and without worrying about grammar and vocabulary. Concentrate on *ideas*. After five minutes, read what you have written. What main idea do you see in your writing? Skip a line and write that main idea in one sentence.

2. Begin with the main idea sentence, and write for five more minutes. Then stop writing and read what you have written. What main idea do you see in your writing now? Skip a line and write that new main idea in one sentence.

3. Write for five more minutes starting with the new main idea sentence. When you finish, read what you have written. Once again, write the new main idea in one sentence.

   Follow-up After looping three times, you will probably have a clear idea of your thesis and of some secondary ideas to support it. If not, you may want to continue looping until a good thesis for your essay emerges.

💬 C Expanding your point of view: Interview

All five of the writing topics in section A can be informed by outside input. Choose someone outside your class to interview about your topic. Select your informant according to the topic you have chosen. For topics 1 and 2, choose someone who works. For topic 3, interview at least one woman. For topic 4, interview a manager. And for topic 5, talk to someone who you consider to be a hard worker.

Follow these steps for the interview:

1 *Interview questions*
Work with other students who have chosen the same topic. Together, write six to eight interview questions that you will ask your informants. Make sure the questions relate directly to your topic.

2 *Interview procedure*
- Introduce yourself and explain the purpose of your interview.
- Use the questions your group decided on.
- Listen attentively to your informant's answers. Ask additional questions if you don't understand fully.
- Summarize what the informant says to show your interest and understanding.
- Write down your informant's exact words if possible.

D Initial drafts

FIRST DRAFT ··

Write an essay on your topic. The essay must include an introduction, body paragraphs, and a conclusion. Keep balance in mind: A good introduction can be about one-fifth of your total paper, but no longer. The conclusion can be shorter, but not so short that it seems abrupt or as if the writer is in a hurry to finish.

For your introduction, you may want to incorporate the summary you wrote of the Maugham story. Or you may want to paraphrase some of the opinions from "Mommy Wars, Part II" or quote the opinions of the person(s) you interviewed. Keep in mind the flow diagram, which moves from general to specific and back to general again (see page 101).

You already have a lot of ideas from the looping exercise and the interview you did in the previous sections. If it is easier, write the body of the essay first, then the introduction, and finally the conclusion. If you write the body before the introduction and conclusion, keep in mind the thesis statement that emerged from the looping exercise to help direct your thinking and writing. Taking the interview into account, do you need to adjust your thesis? Support your thesis statement with your own ideas and/or those from the readings and interview. After you've written your first draft, set your paper aside for several hours or overnight.

REVISION

Look at your first draft through others' eyes by checking it against the criteria listed in the *Essay Assessment Guidelines* on page 112. Revise your paper and label it "Draft 2."

E Review, revision, and assessment

PEER FEEDBACK

Read a classmate's paper, and give feedback using the *Essay Assessment Checklist* on page 112. Write your comments on the checklist, but make no marks on your classmate's paper. Give the checklist and the paper back to the writer. Answer any questions your classmate has about your feedback.

FURTHER REVISION

What did you learn from the feedback you received? Is your essay successful—is it convincing, interesting, clearly organized, and complete? If not, how can you make it more successful?

Revise your paper using the feedback you got in class. Give your teacher all drafts (with the last draft marked "Final draft") and the *Essay Assessment Checklist* completed by your classmate.

Writer's name: _____

Reader's name: _____

Essay Assessment Checklist Chapter 4

These are the criteria for a well-written essay. Use them to examine your writing, or a classmate's, and check *Yes* or *No* for each item. You may wish to add comments or suggestions.

Content and ideas

	Yes	No	Reader's comments
1 The writer has thought carefully about the topic and has a clear thesis.	☐	☐	
2 The writer supports the main points with enough details to give the reader a reason to believe the points.	☐	☐	
3 The writer's voice is clear because he or she writes in a sincere way and keeps the audience in mind.	☐	☐	
4 The reader wants to continue reading to the end. It's interesting.	☐	☐	

Organization and form

	Yes	No	Reader's comments
5 The essay has a clear beginning, middle, and end. There are separate introductory, body, and concluding paragraphs.	☐	☐	
6 The flow is from general to specific and back to general in the conclusion.	☐	☐	
7 The essay moves logically in a straight line. The reader can understand the thesis and support fully after one reading.	☐	☐	

Language

	Yes	No	Reader's comments
8 The paper is easy to understand. These elements are used well:			
• sentence structure	☐	☐	
• grammar	☐	☐	
• vocabulary	☐	☐	
• mechanics (spelling, capitalization, punctuation)	☐	☐	
• coherence from sentence to sentence	☐	☐	

CHAPTER 5

Out of Courtesy

- What kind of manners do these students have?
- What does their behavior tell you about their attitude towards their teacher? Toward other people in general?

PART 1

INTRODUCTION TO THE TOPIC, READING, AND DISCUSSION

A Reflection

Read the situations. Which ones do you think show discourteous behavior, or bad manners? Which ones would upset you? Why? Which would not bother you?

1. When she gets angry, my wife always yells at me.

2. Our boss doesn't appreciate us. He never thanks us for all the work we do even when we work overtime.

3. My teenager is sullen and surly; when I try to talk about what's bothering her, she is silent, bad-tempered, and rude.

4. A friend of mine never returns my phone calls.

5. A young man I know drives very aggressively: he follows too closely, blows his horn constantly, never yields the right of way to other drivers, and doesn't dim his bright lights for oncoming vehicles.

6. When I asked a friend if she liked my new fiancé, she said, "If he were the last man on earth, I wouldn't marry him."

B Discussion

Discuss your answers in pairs, in small groups, or as a class.

C Preparing to read

NOTES ON THE READING

Dr. Norman Vincent Peale, a minister and writer, is known for his inspirational writing on a variety of topics. This magazine article, "Courtesy: Key to a Happier World," shows his conviction, or very strong belief, that the world would be a better place if people were more courteous to each other.

In the first half of the article, Dr. Peale classifies the components of courtesy. In the second half, he gives three pieces of advice on how to improve one's manners. Although his topic is a serious one, Dr. Peale writes about it simply, with down-to-earth examples and anecdotes to illustrate his points; he keeps his large, public audience in mind. As a man of religion, he connects good manners, or courteous behavior, with the Golden Rule: Do unto others as you would have them do unto you. In simpler words, it means you should treat others the way you want to be treated. In this article he refers to the Golden Rule, assuming his audience is familiar with it.

PREVIEWING THE VOCABULARY

Before reading, preview the vocabulary in context. Read these key sentences based on the text, and choose the best meaning for the underlined words.

1 "I hate my boss," a grim-faced office worker muttered. "He never shows appreciation for anything."
   a. amused-looking
   b. unhappy-looking
   c. secretive-looking and afraid

2 What are the basic ingredients of good manners? A strong sense of justice is one; courtesy is often nothing more than a highly developed sense of fair play.
   a. one's self
   b. compassion
   c. right behavior or treatment

3 A man dining alone was trying to unscrew the cap of a bottle of catsup, but his fingers were so badly crippled by arthritis that he couldn't do it.
   a. cut
   b. polished
   c. weakened; damaged

4 The busboy feigned great effort to open the bottle even though he could have done it with no effort at all.
   a. needed
   b. tried to hide his
   c. pretended to use

5 What impelled the boy to take so much trouble to spare the feelings of a stranger?
   a. caused him to take
   b. confused him about taking
   c. prevented him from taking

6 Yet another component of politeness is the capacity to treat all people alike, regardless of their status or importance.
   a. ability
   b. room
   c. unwillingness

7 One difficult but essential thing to remember is to refuse to let other people's bad manners goad you into retaliating in kind.
   a. serve as an example of good behavior
   b. cause you to do the same harm in return
   c. convince you to do something kind

8 If your thoughts are <u>predominantly self-directed</u>, a discourteous person is what you will be.
   a. usually about others
   b. mainly about yourself
   c. seldom about yourself

9 In the intimacy of the home, it is easy to <u>displace</u> disappointment, frustration, or anger onto the nearest person, and that person is often a husband or wife.
   a. hide
   b. make disappear
   c. inappropriately direct or aim

10 To have good manners you must be able to accept courtesy, receive it gladly, and <u>rejoice</u> when it comes your way.
    a. not care
    b. be very happy
    c. be very suspicious

11 Strangely, some people are suspicious of gracious treatment. They suspect the other person of having <u>some ulterior motive</u>.
    a. a big heart
    b. a hidden reason
    c. complete honesty

12 But some of the most precious gifts in life come <u>with no strings attached</u>. You can't achieve a beautiful day through any effort on your part.
    a. without any conditions
    b. with no possibility of happening
    c. wrapped in paper but without any ribbon

13 Life is full of minor irritations and <u>trials</u> and injustices.
    a. problems
    b. opportunities
    c. chances for revenge

14 I think that if I were allowed to add one small <u>beatitude</u> as a footnote to these other lessons, it might be: Blessed are the courteous.
    a. warning
    b. anecdote
    c. blessing or declaration

Follow-up Check and discuss your answers in pairs or with the class.

D Reading for overall meaning

Read the article at a quick but comfortable pace. As you read, think about this question:

Does Dr. Peale feel good manners are more a matter of (1) how we look at ourselves or (2) how we look at other people?

Courtesy: Key to a Happier World

Dr. Norman Vincent Peale

Many years ago trying to help people with every kind of trouble left me with one sure conviction: In case after case the difficulty could have been overcome—or might never have arisen—if the people involved had just treated one another with common courtesy.

Courtesy, politeness, good manners—call it what you will, the supply never seems to equal the demand. "It's not so much what my husband says," a tearful wife confides, "as the way he says it. Why does he have to yell at me?" "I hate my boss," a grim-faced office worker mutters. "He never shows appreciation for anything." "All we get from our teenagers," a harassed parent says, "is a sullen surliness."

Such complaints are not limited to people who sit in my study. Human beings everywhere hunger for courtesy. "Good manners," said Ralph Waldo Emerson, "are the happy way of doing things." And the reverse is equally true. Bad manners can ruin a day—or wreck a friendship.

What are the basic ingredients of good manners? Certainly a strong sense of justice is one; courtesy is often nothing more than a highly developed sense of fair play. A friend once told me of driving along a one-lane, unpaved mountain road. Ahead was another car that produced clouds of choking dust, and it was a long way to the nearest paved highway. Suddenly, at a wider place, the car ahead pulled off the road. Thinking that its owner might have engine trouble, my friend stopped and asked if anything was wrong. "No," said the other driver. "But you've endured my dust this far; I'll put up with yours the rest of the way." There was a man with manners, and an innate sense of fair play.

Another ingredient of courtesy is empathy, a quality that enables a person to see into the mind or heart of someone else, to understand the pain or unhappiness there and to do something to minimize it. Recently in a book about a famous restaurant chain I came across such an episode.

A man dining alone was trying to unscrew the cap of a bottle of catsup, but his fingers were so badly crippled by arthritis that he couldn't do it. He asked a young busboy to help him. The boy took the bottle, turned his back momentarily and loosened the cap without difficulty. Then he tightened it again.

continued

Turning back to the man, he feigned a great effort to open the bottle without success. Finally he took it into the kitchen and returned shortly, saying that he had managed to loosen it—but only with a pair of pliers. What impelled the boy to take so much trouble to spare the feelings of a stranger? Courtesy, compassionate courtesy.

Yet another component of politeness is the capacity to treat all people alike, regardless of all status or importance. Even when you have doubts about some people, act as if they are worthy of your best manners. You may also be astonished to find out that they really are.

I truly believe that anyone can improve his or her manners by doing three things. First, by practicing courtesy. All skills require constant repetition to become second nature; good manners are no exception.

One simple way is to concentrate on your performance in a specific area for about a week. Telephone manners, for example. How often do you talk too long, speak abruptly, fail to identify yourself, keep people waiting, display impatience with the operator or fail to return a call? Or driving a car, why not monitor yourself sternly for aggressive driving, unnecessary horn-blowing, following too closely, failing to yield the right-of-way?

One difficult but essential thing to remember is to refuse to let other people's bad manners goad you into retaliating in kind. I recall a story told by a young man who was in a car with his father one night when a driver in an oncoming vehicle failed to dim his lights. "Give him the brights, Dad!" the young man urged in exasperation. "Son," replied the father, "that driver is certainly discourteous and probably stupid. But if I give him the brights he'll be discourteous, stupid, and *blind*—and that's a combination I don't want to tangle with!"

The second requirement for improving your manners is to think in a courteous way. In the long run, the kind of person you are is the result of what you've been thinking over the past twenty or thirty years. If your thoughts are predominantly self-directed, a discourteous person is what you will be. If on the other hand you train yourself to be considerate of others, if you can acquire the habit of identifying with their problems and hopes and fears, good manners will follow almost automatically.

Nowhere is thinking courtesy more important than in marriage. In the intimacy of the home it is easy to displace disappointment or frustration or anger onto the nearest person, and that person is often a husband or wife.

"When you feel your anger getting out of control," I have often said to married couples, "force yourself for the next ten minutes to treat your married partner as if he or she were a guest in your home." I knew that if they could impose just ten minutes of good manners on themselves, the worst of the storm would blow over.

Finally, to have good manners you must be able to accept courtesy, receive it gladly, rejoice when it comes your way. Strangely, some people are suspicious of gracious treatment. They suspect the other person of having some ulterior motive.

continued

But some of the most precious gifts in life come with no strings attached. You can't achieve a beautiful day through any effort on your part. You can't buy a sunset or even the scent of a rose. Those are the world's courtesies to us, offered with love and no thought of reward or return. Good manners are, or should be, like that.

In the end, it all comes down to how you regard people—not just people in general, but individuals. Life is full of minor irritations and trials and injustices. The only constant, daily, effective solution is politeness—which is the golden rule in action. I think that if I were allowed to add one small beatitude as a footnote to the other it might be: Blessed are the courteous.

Follow-up Now answer this question:

Does Dr. Peale feel good manners are more a matter of (1) how we look at ourselves or (2) how we look at other people?

E Reading for more detail

Read the selection a second time. Use the questions to read for more detail and to bring your experience to the reading.

1 Which of the three "basic ingredients" of courtesy makes the most sense to you?

2 Would people in your country agree with Dr. Peale's "main ingredients" of good manners?

3 Which of Dr. Peale's ways of improving manners would you find the most difficult to follow? Why?

4 The writer uses anecdotes to illustrate his points. Which anecdote will you remember?

5 *Key words* Make a list of six key words or expressions that you feel are important to the article. Be ready to explain what each word means and why it is important.

Follow-up Discuss your answers in pairs, in small groups, or as a class.

PART 2
PERSONAL WRITTEN RESPONSE

A Journals: A private audience

Choose two of the following topics. Write for about 20 minutes in your journal notebook. These journal entries are for your eyes only, so do not spend a lot of time using a dictionary or worrying about grammar.

1. Think of an incident in which someone was very rude to you. What did that person do? How did you feel? How did you react?

2. Do you feel that you have good manners? Do people think of you as a polite person? Explain.

3. Give an example of something rude that you have done. Why did you do it?

B Shared writing

Choose two of the following topics, and write for a total of 20 minutes. Your audience is your classmates, with whom you will share your writing. They will be interested not only in what you feel but also in why you feel that way. Express your views clearly and support them.

1. Every culture/religion has its own golden rule that people try to live by. What is yours? How do people apply it?

2. Dr. Peale tells us that our manners depend on how we regard other people. Do they also depend on how we regard ourselves?

3. Do you agree with Dr. Peale that our lives would be happier if we all had better manners? Explain.

C Feedback on your writing

Get feedback on how clear and logical your thinking and writing are. Select one of the questions from *Shared Writing,* and read your answer to a small group of classmates. Follow the *Peer Feedback Guidelines* on page 11.

PART 3
FURTHER READING, WRITING, AND DISCUSSION

- Will this grandmother tell her granddaughter how she really feels about her appearance?
- Should the grandmother keep silent?

A Preparing to read

NOTES ON THE READING

In this article author Donald McCullough surprises us when he tells us it is sometimes good manners to tell lies. He describes a time when he told the truth. He realizes now that a lie would have *saved a lot of grief* and prevented a lot of trouble. He also recommends that we lie to certain kinds of people, for example people who tend to *distort* the truth, misrepresenting what they hear. McCullough makes it clear he is speaking about *white lies:* social lies, lies we tell to *spare someone's feelings.* The author does not approve of more serious lies, which he calls "gray" or "black" lies and finds *morally unacceptable.*

(*Note:* Words in italics are from the article.)

REFLECTION AND DISCUSSION ....

Read each situation. Would you tell a white lie (stretch the truth) or tell the truth? Write *WL* for a white lie, *T* for the truth.

_____ 1 A friend is visiting with his newborn baby. You think the baby is extremely ugly. The friend asks you if you think the baby is beautiful.

_____ 2 Your sister is going to elope* with a man your parents don't like. She shares this secret with you in confidence. One day your mother asks you if you know why your sister has been acting so secretively lately.

_____ 3 Your friend Mike is having trouble with his boss and is thinking of quitting his job. Another friend, who you know is a blabbermouth* (with an unrelenting and undiscriminating tongue*), asks if you have heard anything about Mike's "situation."

_____ 4 Your aunt has just lost her job because she is suffering from depression. You run into a very good friend of hers who always has your aunt's best interests at heart.* The friend asks you how your aunt is doing.

_____ 5 You run into another friend of your aunt's who is known for speaking very frankly about people. She often tells the truth in order to belittle or demean* people. The friend asks you how your aunt is doing.

_____ 6 A cousin who has very low self-esteem asks if you think he would be a good doctor. Your honest opinion is that he would make a very poor doctor.

belittle or demean (someone): *speak unkindly to reduce the value of a person or the respect he/she is given*
blabbermouth: *a person who reveals secrets by talking too much*
elope: *run away to get married secretly instead of having a traditional wedding*
have someone's best interests at heart: *act for someone's advantage, to help*
unrelenting and undiscriminating tongue: *a person who talks without stopping and without thought*

Follow-up Discuss your answers in pairs, in small groups, or as a class.

B Reading for overall meaning

Read this selection the first time to answer this question:

Does McCullough give us an easy formula for knowing the difference between appropriate white lies and morally unacceptable lies?

Tell White Lies (Occasionally)
Protecting from Unnecessary Hurt

by Donald W. McCullough

Verna claims that I said her baby was ugly. I can't imagine being that insensitive, though it was a long time ago and my memory isn't exact in these matters. I do recall Verna holding up her newborn and saying, "Isn't she cute?" And I, seeing a splotchy, scrunched little face and being committed to complete honesty, must have said something like, "Well, she really is . . . a baby?" Or maybe, "It takes an infant a few months before she can really be considered cute." Or I suppose there is a small possibility I said, "Strictly speaking, she is kind of ugly at the moment but will undoubtedly become a ravishing beauty."

Nearly thirty years have passed, but whenever I run into Verna she reminds me that I called her baby ugly. I don't know her daughter; for all I know she became Miss Universe or perhaps my words lodged in her tiny subconscious and she has spent the last fifteen years in psychoanalysis working on low self-esteem. In any event, I now wish I had lied. It would have saved all of us a lot of grief.

Occasionally, courtesy calls for a lie. Let me hasten to stress I'm talking about white lies, not black or gray or even off-white lies. Snow-white lies. But even so, I realize I've just launched this chapter into very dangerous waters, with tough ethical questions all around us. We had better navigate through this subject very carefully, with a firm grip on the tiller. . . .

. . . How can we speak truthfully about lying? The ancient philosopher Aristotle may be of help to us. He said that honesty was more than unloading everything to everyone. Rather, it is speaking the right truth to the right person at the right time in the right way for the right reason.

Not every truth is mine to tell: a truth shared in confidence and a truth that would needlessly hurt another is not mine to tell. Not every person has a right to know the truth. Some willfully distort what they hear; some use facts to cover a larger, more important truth: some have blabbermouths with unrelenting and undiscriminating tongues. Not every time is appropriate for the truth: some seasons call for tactful silence: the day your friend's daughter dropped out of school is not the day to tell her about your daughter making the honor roll. Not every way of communicating honors the truth. Sometimes the manner in which something is said subverts reality, as when a preacher says all the right words about God's love but through a tone of voice and a concluding string of "oughts" (therefore we ought to do this and we ought to do that) that makes you feel guiltier than ever. Not every reason deserves the use of truth: some motives for telling the truth are simply too destructive to deserve the respectability of being clothed in the truth. Some expressions of "honesty" are really attempts to demean and belittle another person.

When it's the wrong truth or the wrong person or the wrong time or the wrong way or the wrong reason, a white lie may have more integrity

continued

than a facile, insensitive "honesty." But when does a white lie begin to turn a slight shade of gray? When does it cross over and become an immoral act of dishonesty?

Perhaps a good test would be to ask, Does this lie protect the other person or does it protect me? Let's waste no time in admitting that it's not easy to tell the difference. On the surface, a lie may appear to protect another person from unnecessary pain; on closer examination, however, it's actually an attempt to save me from uncomfortable exposure. In Graham Greene's *The Heart of the Matter,* a police officer in a West African colony during the war has an affair, and in an effort to "protect" his wife from the pain of the truth, walks down a road of falsehood that leads to disaster. Greene's story may be fiction but it's a profound truth reenacted everyday. It's easy to convince ourselves we're guarding the feelings of another when we're only trying to protect ourselves—and this sort of deception often ends in more complication and more lying and more pain than we could have ever imagined.

But just because it's difficult to tell the difference between an appropriate lie and a morally unacceptable lie does not mean we give up the attempt to make the distinction. Life, after all, is difficult. So we press on, doing our best, knowing we're not God, and counting on the grace of God when we blow it. Though committed to honesty, we know that sometimes courtesy calls for creative stretching of the truth.

Follow-up Now answer the question:

Does McCullough give us an easy formula for knowing the difference between appropriate white lies and morally unacceptable lies?

C Reading for more detail

Read the selection again. Mark any places in the text that are still unclear to you.

D Helping each other understand

Write for about 20 minutes about this selection. Write about one or more of the questions below.

1. What do you have trouble understanding?
2. Think of a white lie you told recently. What did you say, and why didn't you tell the truth?
3. Were you convinced by the author's explanation of "appropriate" white lies?

Follow-up To a small group of students, read what you have written. Read your reaction a second time if necessary. Each group member will respond with (1) a question, (2) a comment, and/or (3) help with what you didn't understand.

E Discussion: Critical thinking

Discuss these questions in pairs, in small groups, or as a class.

1. Would Peale approve or disapprove of McCullough's ideas on white lies? Explain.

2. Imagine that you were turned down for a job that you wanted very badly. Would you rather hear the unpleasant truth about why you were rejected or a tactful lie? Explain.

3. Mark Twain, writer and humorist, said this about lying: "One of the most striking differences between a cat and a lie is that a cat has only nine lives." What do you think this quotation means?

4. Are there universal good manners? In other words, is there a core of good manners that polite people of all countries recognize? Or are good manners different for each individual culture?

PART 4
FOCUS ON WRITING SKILLS

A Meeting reader expectations: Outlining

Effective writing is well organized, making it easy for the reader to grasp the main idea and follow the logic of the writer's points. Before writing a draft, making an outline is a good way to organize one's thinking by giving ideas order and priority. If the order and priority of the ideas in one's writing are clear, it will be clear to readers which ideas are main points and which are secondary points.

In Exercise 1 you will complete an outline of Peale's article, "Courtesy: Key to a Happier World." As you do the exercise, keep in mind that:

- Ideas with Roman numerals (I, II, etc.) are the most general. Roman numerals I and II express the main points of Peale's article.
- Ideas with capital letters (A, B, etc.) are more specific and support the ideas with Roman numerals directly above them.
- Ideas with Arabic numerals (1, 2, etc.) are even more specific and support the more general ideas directly above them.

EXERCISE 1 *Completing an outline*

Complete the outline using information from the reading.

Thesis: Life's difficulties would be minimized if people were more courteous to each other.

I. Basic ingredients of good manners

　A. Justice

　B. _____

　C. _____

II. Three ways to improve one's manners

　A. Practice courtesy

　　1. _____

　　2. Don't let others' bad manners make you rude

　B. _____

　C. Be able to accept courtesy

Conclusion: Politeness is the golden rule in action.

B Using another's writing: Summarizing an article

In academic writing it is common practice to refer to another author's writing. This can be an effective way to support a thesis, or strengthen an argument, but only if it is done honestly and skillfully. You can use another's writing honestly and skillfully if you (1) mention the author's name, and (2) summarize the author's message in a few words.

EXERCISE 2 *Summarizing Peale's main points*

Working from the outline you prepared in Exercise 1, summarize the main points of the two parts of Peale's article: the three components of courtesy and the three ways to improve one's manners. Limit yourself to about 75 words. Begin as shown:

In "Courtesy: Key to a Happier World," Dr. Peale lists the three components of courtesy and . . .

Revise your draft to make your summary clear, concise, and grammatical.

Follow-up In small groups exchange summaries and read them aloud. Discuss similarities and differences.

EXERCISE 3 *A student essay*

Before you read this essay by a Mexican student, preview the questions at the end of the essay on page 129. Keep them in mind as you read.

Adanari Navarro

Teaching the Golden Rule

The behavior of individuals is very complicated; it is influenced by heredity, environment, and culture. Culture includes rules of how an individual is expected to behave in a particular society. Sometimes rules for behavior differ from one culture to another, and sometimes the rules are similar. What is meant by the "golden rule" in the United States and in Mexico is very similar, if not in words, in sentiment. In the United States, the golden rule is "Do unto others as you would have them do unto you." This instructs people how to behave with others inside and outside the home. The Mexican golden rule, "Between individuals, as between nations, respect for other people's rights means peace," likewise instructs people how to behave with others. Perhaps because all cultures are equally concerned about their children's manners, we find many more similarities than differences in the way Mexicans and Americans teach children the golden rule.

continued

Children in both cultures first learn the golden rule of their country inside the home. Inside the family is where children learn their culture and where they learn to behave. In both the United States and Mexico, parents teach their children how to respect other people and, as a consequence, to receive respect from others. At home, siblings are taught to take care of each other's belongings. Furthermore, they are taught not to call each other names or hurt each other's feelings. They are also taught to trust each other and their parents by always telling the truth. Parents teach the golden rule to avoid quarrels and misunderstandings among the members of the family. Children learn how to treat others by learning how to apply the golden rule with family members.

When children get older, they go to school, and the parents have to teach them how to get along with other children and adults at school. Mothers in both cultures worry about this adjustment and think of ways to apply the golden rule. They expect their children to make friends at school, so they may tell their children to respect others by not taking their belongings. They will tell their children to be good students and follow the teacher's instructions. Mothers also remind children that, like at home, they should not call other children names or hurt anyone's feelings. Finally, if other children do not treat them with respect, or cause them trouble, children are told to avoid fights by going to the teacher and telling the truth.

As part of their upbringing, children are also taught to respect neighbors, but the golden rule as it applies to neighbors is different in Mexico from in the United States. Among Mexican families, it is very common to offer help when a new family comes to live in the neighborhood. Mexicans offer their help in moving or by lending equipment like ladders or tools. If it is needed, some people will even offer food to their new neighbors. However, American families apply the golden rule by not getting in anyone's way. They do try to make friends with the neighbors and offer support, but they will be careful about interfering in the beginning, perhaps because they are more independent and expect others to be or perhaps because people move more often in the United States. This difference in relations between neighbors, which children learn by example from their parents, may explain why neighbors in Mexico are more likely to become friends than they are in the United States.

In the case of strangers, the golden rule is applied similarly and differently in the two countries. In American culture, the family emphasizes independence and teaches children how to take care of themselves. This lesson often includes a warning that they can't trust everyone and should be careful with strangers. Children are taught what to do, how to use the phone, and whom to call for help in case of emergency or trouble with a stranger, for example. Although Mexicans are not as wary of strangers, they also tell their children to be careful of them and to tell an adult if help is needed. Mexicans may not need to warn their children about strangers quite as much as Americans do simply because

continued

children, who are more dependent in Mexico, are with their parents most of the time. Possibly because independence is not as big a cultural value in Mexico as in the United States, people give and accept help more readily. Children, then, are taught to help elderly people and pregnant women, for example, by helping them to cross the street or to carry a parcel. 60

In both the Mexican and the American cultures, parents want their children to have good manners. Parents teach the golden rule in order to have peace at home, to guide children's behavior in school, and to teach children to respect the neighbors and how to deal with strangers. The similarities in teaching the golden rule in both cultures exist because of the common concern of parents to 65 teach good manners. The differences are not as relevant but stand out because of the differences between the two cultures.

Answer the questions.

1. What is Ms. Navarro's thesis? Which sentence is her thesis statement?
2. How many support paragraphs did she write? What is the main idea of each one?
3. Is the paper logically organized? Is it clear which are her main ideas and how secondary ideas support them?
4. Does each body paragraph support her thesis?
5. What is her goal in the conclusion? Do we know how she feels about the similarities and differences between the two cultures?

Complete the outline of paragraph 4.

I. The golden rule as it applies to neighbors is different in Mexico from in the United States.

    A. Mexicans _____

        1. _____

        2. _____

        3. _____

    B. Americans _____

        1. _____

        2. _____

            a. _____

            b. _____

Conclusion: _____

ⓒ Sentence grammar: Sentence variety

A writer who uses the same kind of sentence over and over produces boring writing. Using diverse sentence types adds interest and variety to writing. Writers achieve variety by using three sentence types: simple, compound, and complex.

SIMPLE AND COMPOUND SENTENCES ································

A *simple sentence* has one independent clause. A *compound sentence* has two or more independent clauses usually joined by a comma and a coordinating conjunction (*and, or, but, so, for, nor, yet*).

Look at the sentences below. Identify the subject of each verb.

SIMPLE   a. My houseguests returned from a long day of shopping and went straight to bed.

COMPOUND   b. My house guests returned home from a long day of shopping, and we decided to stay at home instead of going out.

                  c. I had a lot of homework, but I didn't study that night.

EXERCISE 4 *Distinguishing compound from simple sentences*

In the blanks write *C* for a compound sentence and *S* for a simple sentence.

_____ 1 John didn't show up for his philosophy test or notify the teacher.

_____ 2 The teacher was upset with John, but she allowed him to schedule a make-up test because of his excuse.

_____ 3 He had missed the test because of a death in the family and he had also missed three days of class.

_____ 4 With extra time to study, John did better on the test than most of the other students.

_____ 5 One student with a low grade thought this was unfair and complained to the teacher.

_____ 6 At first, the teacher wasn't sure how to handle the situation, but a solution soon occurred to her.

_____ 7 To John's dismay, she took ten points away from him for taking the test late.

_____ 8 John may have been disappointed, but the other students felt better.

MORE ON COMPOUND SENTENCES ································

Most compound sentences are formed by joining two independent clauses with a comma and a coordinating conjunction such as *and, or, but,* or *so*. The coordinating conjunctions *for, nor,* and *yet* occur almost exclusively in writing, so they add a level of formality. Look at the examples on the next page.

a. Fred is quite good-looking, *yet* he doesn't think so.

b. The students were unhappy with their professor, *for* he often wasted their time in class.

c. I'm not going to the party, *nor* do I plan to inform the hostess.

d. I didn't offer to show my driver's license to the police, *nor* did they ask for it.

Note that in example *a, yet* is used as a coordinating conjunction with the same meaning as *but*. In example *b, for* means *because*. In examples *c* and *d, nor* continues the negative meaning from the previous clause. The word order of the subject and verb is inverted after *nor*.

A compound sentence can also consist of two independent clauses joined with a semicolon and a transition word.

a. The teacher treats them with respect; *therefore,* the students try to live up to her expectations.

b. Don't lie to me; *then* I won't lie to you.

EXERCISE 5 *Writing compound sentences*

Form compound sentences by adding an independent clause (with a subject and verb).

1 Did they treat you courteously, or _____?

2 The students respect that teacher, for _____.

3 I wanted to tell the truth, yet _____.

4 _____, so I told a white lie.

5 _____, but I was suspicious of their motives.

6 _____, and another is empathy.

7 _____, nor should you fail to return a person's phone call.

8 _____, so their children will probably have very good manners.

9 _____, for the thoughts in your mind determine the kind of person you are.

10 _____, nor is he very tactful.

COMPLEX SENTENCES

A *complex sentence* has a dependent clause plus one or more independent clauses. The dependent clause is introduced by a subordinating conjunction (*because, although, since, if, whenever, even though, so that, in that,* and so on), which explains the relationship between the two clauses. If the dependent clause comes first, it is followed by a comma.

a. *Since we got to the concert late,* we had to make our way to our seats in the dark.
   b. We left class early *so that we could attend a special lecture.*
   c. Her car is different from mine *in that her sports car needs more expensive repairs and more fuel.*
   d. *When I went home,* my roommate wasn't there, so I started to cook dinner.

(*Note:* The subordinating conjunction *so that* communicates purpose and often occurs with *can/could* or *will/would*. The subordinating conjunction *in that* means "for the reason that" or "because."

EXERCISE 6 *Writing complex sentences*

Add an independent clause to each dependent clause to make a complex sentence.

1 _____ *even though* John's rude remark made me angry.

2 _____ *since* he lied to me last year.

3 *Whenever* someone is rude to me, _____.

4 _____ *because* he is considerate of others.

5 _____ *so that* they will treat me courteously, too.

6 *If* a person's bad manners bother you, _____.

7 *Although* I try to think in a courteous way, _____.

8 _____ *even when* they are treated discourteously.

9 *If* people practice courtesy, _____.

10 *Because* Mr. Vann is suspicious of others' motives, _____.

EXERCISE 7 *Distinguishing simple, compound, and complex sentences*

In the blanks write *S* for a simple sentence, *C* for a compound sentence, and *CX* for a complex sentence.

_____ 1 Joe is not going to take a vacation during spring break because of an assignment to earn extra credit in his economics class.

_____ 2 He has to write two long papers, and it will take him the whole spring holiday.

_____ 3 Because the library has reduced hours during break, Joe will have to work mostly at home.

_____ 4 With little knowledge of the topics, he will have to do a lot of research.

_____ 5   The library's computerized indexing system will make his research fairly easy.

_____ 6   He will try to finish his research by the middle of the week; then he can spend the rest of the week writing the papers.

_____ 7   A friend has volunteered to type the papers if they are finished by Saturday.

_____ 8   Joe will do all he can to finish by Saturday so that he can take advantage of his friend's help.

_____ 9   He has to finish on time, or he'll have to type the paper himself.

_____ 10 Joe has decided never to miss another vacation because of schoolwork.

LONG RAMBLING SENTENCES

Long strings of independent clauses joined by coordinating conjunctions can leave the reader confused and frustrated. These long rambling sentences are also perceived as informal because they seem more like speaking than writing.

Compare these two versions of the same paragraph:

(1)   I went home, but my roommate wasn't there, so I started to cook dinner, but my roommate came in and saw me trying to cook his favorite recipe, but I didn't really know how to make it well, and he got really angry, so I stopped cooking, and he made dinner for us, and then everything was all right.

(2)   When I went home, my roommate wasn't there, so I started to cook dinner. Then, my roommate came in. He saw me trying to cook his favorite recipe even though I didn't know how to make it well. I stopped cooking because he got really angry. In the end, he made dinner for us, and everything was all right.

The compound structure of version 1 is easier to write, perhaps, but not very satisfying to read. Version 2 has more coherence and interest because the writer took the time to think and make decisions about the importance of each clause and its relationship to the others. The use of simple and complex sentences, as well as compound sentences, also makes version 2 more interesting to read.

EXERCISE 8   *Editing rambling sentences for sentence variety*

Rewrite the long rambling sentences in the paragraph on the next page into several shorter, more coherent and clearer ones. Use subordinating conjunctions, transition words, and simple sentences in place of some of the coordinating conjunctions to achieve variety in sentence type.

The telephone rang, and I answered, and I heard the voice of my wife's best friend, Gladys, and her voice was so sweet and sugary, so I knew she thinks I'm a jerk, but that's all right because I can't stand her either, but my wife was out, so I had to talk to Gladys, and she said she had invited my wife and me to dinner on Friday, but my wife wasn't sure if I was free, so here's Gladys calling again and I would rather watch basketball on TV and not eat than spend time with her and her boring husband, but I said, "We'd be glad to come to dinner. I look forward to seeing you and Ted on Friday." Yes, I lied, but it wasn't a bad lie because it's the kind you tell to make social relationships smoother, and I realize the lie hid my feelings, but it also protected a larger truth—that my wife really will look forward to the evening because she loves Gladys, and Gladys' life is full of problems right now, and I love my wife and want to make her happy, so in the interest of this larger truth, lying was the courteous thing to do.

(Adapted from Say Please, Say Thank You, *by Donald W. McCullough)*

PART 5
FORMAL WRITING ASSIGNMENT

A Writing topics

Choose a topic for your essay from the list below.

1. *Comparison and contrast* Compare your culture's golden rule to the Biblical one: "Do unto others as you would have them do unto you."

2. Choose one of these quotations to write about:

   "Happiness is when what you think, what you say, and what you do are in harmony." *(Mohandas K. Gandhi, Hindu religious leader and social reformer)*

   "If you do not tell the truth about yourself, you cannot tell it about other people." *(Virginia Woolf, British author)*

3. Think back to the discussion on page 125 about universal manners. Answer these questions in your essay: Are there universal good manners? In other words, is there a core of good manners that polite people of all countries recognize? Or are good manners different for each individual culture?

B Generating ideas: Free writing

Write freely on your topic for 20 minutes. Then read what you have written. Write down three questions about the topic that you would like to discuss with classmates.

 Follow-up Meet in a small group with other students who have chosen the same topic. Share your questions with each other. Then write six interview questions to ask an informant outside your class.

C Expanding your point of view: Interview

Conduct an interview with an informant outside your class. Use the interview questions your group wrote in *Generating Ideas: Free Writing*. Follow these steps:

1. Explain your purpose in interviewing, listen attentively, and try to summarize orally what your informant says.

2. Ask additional questions if you are not sure you understand what your informant has said.

3. Take notes during the interview, but also try to maintain eye contact with your informant.

4. Take down the informant's name and other relevant personal data that you might use in your essay.

D Initial drafts

OUTLINE ··

In Parts 1–3 of this chapter, you thought, read, discussed, and wrote as a way to develop ideas on the topic. In Part 5 you have done additional free writing and conducted an interview to help you think about your essay topic. To help select the best ideas and organize your thoughts, prepare an outline similar to the one in Part 4, Exercise 1 (page 126). Follow these steps:

1. Write a thesis statement to help you choose the best ideas to use for support.

2. Decide on your main points of support. These points can be developed into the topic sentences for your body paragraphs.

3. For each body paragraph, outline the ideas you will use to support each main point.

4. If an idea comes to you for a conclusion, add it to your outline.

Your thesis

I. Main point of support

    A. Supporting idea

    B. Supporting idea

FIRST DRAFT ··

Write the first draft from your outline. Give your writing your own voice, your mark. To do this, consider the following:

- Use a true personal anecdote (for example, in the introduction), or use other real examples from your experience in the body paragraphs.
- Choose examples that will appeal to your audience.
- If you use another person's ideas, connect the ideas to your own experience. (Identify the author or informant in your essay.)

REVISION ··

Look at your first draft through others' eyes by checking it against the criteria listed in the *Essay Assessment Guidelines* on page 138. Revise your paper and mark it "Draft 2."

E Review, revision, and assessment

PEER FEEDBACK

Read a classmate's paper and give feedback using the *Essay Assessment Checklist* on page 138. Write your comments on the checklist, but make no marks on your classmate's paper. Give the checklist and the paper back to the writer. Answer any questions your classmate has about your feedback.

FURTHER REVISION

What did you learn from the feedback you received? Is your essay successful—is it convincing, interesting, clearly organized, and complete? If not, how can you make it more successful?

Revise your paper using the feedback you got in class. Give your teacher all drafts (with the last draft marked "Final draft") and the *Essay Assessment Checklist* completed by your classmate.

Writer's name: _____

Reader's name: _____

Essay Assessment Checklist Chapter 5

These are the criteria for a well-written essay. Use them to examine your writing, or a classmate's, and check *Yes* or *No* for each item. You may wish to add comments or suggestions.

Content and ideas

	Yes	No	Reader's comments
1 The writer has thought carefully about the topic and has a clear thesis.	☐	☐	
2 The writer supports the main points enough to give the reader a reason to believe them.	☐	☐	
3 The writer's voice is clear because he or she writes in a sincere way and keeps the audience in mind.	☐	☐	
4 The reader wants to continue reading to the end. It's interesting.	☐	☐	

Organization and form

5 The paper has a clear beginning, middle, and end. There are separate introductory, body, and concluding paragraphs.	☐	☐	
6 The paper is logically organized and the ideas are in a logical order. It's clear which are the main ideas and how other ideas support them.	☐	☐	

Language

7 The paper is easy to understand. These elements are used well:			
• sentence structure	☐	☐	
• grammar	☐	☐	
• vocabulary	☐	☐	
• mechanics (spelling, capitalization, punctuation)	☐	☐	
• coherence from sentence to sentence	☐	☐	
• sentence variety	☐	☐	

CHAPTER 6

Questions of Right and Wrong

- Is the driver of the Winnebago going to stop and help? Or is he going to flee from the scene of this tragedy?
- What would you do in this situation?

PART 1

INTRODUCTION TO THE TOPIC, READING, AND DISCUSSION

A Reflection

All of us must make judgments about right and wrong, or distinguish between moral and immoral behavior. Read these quotations about morality and moral duty. Which quotation makes the most sense to you? The least sense?

1 "If you don't like the way the world is, you change it. You have an obligation to change it. You just do it one step at a time." (*Marian Wright Edelman, president of the Children's Defense Fund and author of* The Measure of Our Success)

2 "We live in a world which is full of misery and ignorance, and the plain duty of each and all of us is to try to make the little corner he can influence somewhat less miserable and somewhat less ignorant than it was before he entered it." *(Thomas Huxley, English biologist and writer)*

3 "We may pretend that we're basically moral people who make mistakes, but the whole of history proves otherwise." *(Terry Hands, British theater and opera director)*

4 "By protecting oneself [e.g., morally], one protects others; by protecting others, one protects oneself." (*from the Buddhist* Samyukta Nikaya)

B Discussion

Where do our ideas about morality come from? Read the following statements. Mark each statement *A* if you agree, *D* if you disagree, and *NS* if you are not sure. Then discuss your answers in pairs or as a class.

_____ 1 My ideas about right and wrong come primarily from my parents and other family members.

_____ 2 Different cultures have different ideas about what makes a person moral.

_____ 3 Religion is the most important source of moral principles for a culture.

_____ 4 Morality is a legacy,* which passes from one generation to the next.

_____ 5 People in politics and business tend to be less moral than other people.

_____ 6 Morality is a personal matter; each person really decides for herself or himself what good and bad behavior is.

legacy: *something that is passed on from those who came before*

_____ 7 Although we inherit a moral legacy from our ancestors, we must adapt this morality to fit our modern lives.

_____ 8 "You are your brother's keeper."

Preparing to read

NOTES ON THE READING

In this selection David Shapiro takes a close look at the *moral legacy* we leave future generations, that is, the moral lessons that we will be remembered by. He writes about a trip he took with his father and a friend in a Winnebago, a huge expensive motor home. During the trip, a tragic incident at a national park leads him to look at his culture and wonder about people's failure to take personal action in an emergency. Looking back at the incident many years later, he remembers two gas stations located at the entrance to the park. He views the two stations as a *metaphor* for the divisions in society. The clean, modern, safe but more expensive gas station is a *corporate franchise,* one branch of thousands owned by a major oil company. The other is poor, dirty, and falling to pieces. Which of the two gas stations do you think is struck by tragedy in the story—the *affluent* franchise or the poor, independent one?

(*Note:* Words in italics are from the reading.)

PREVIEWING THE VOCABULARY

Before reading, preview the vocabulary in context. Read these sentences based on the text and choose the best meaning for the underlined words.

1. We have completed filling our vehicle's huge 32-gallon tank, have <u>stocked up on</u> peanuts and gum, and paid.
   a. checked our supply of
   b. eaten our entire supply of
   c. purchased a good supply of

2. Just as my father angles the Winnebago onto the road, an explosion rocks the gas station. Through the corner of my window, I see a fireball <u>engulf</u> its white clapboard office.
   a. hit
   b. surround
   c. rise above

3. In his nervousness, his jaw is <u>clenched</u> and his hands are tight around the steering wheel.
   a. open
   b. relaxed
   c. closed tightly

4. I see many similarities between this <u>microcosmic</u> memory and the <u>macrocosmic</u> legacy we as a people will leave behind.
   a. small / larger
   b. very old / more current
   c. important / unimportant

5. Bhopal, Chernobyl, the Marshall Islands—time and time again, less-developed places <u>bear the brunt of</u> the technology that sustains more developed ones.
   a. never receive
   b. suffer the bad effects of
   c. have to wait a long time for

6. Were its owners <u>cutting corners on safety</u> in order to keep up with their corporate-supported competitor across the street?
   a. posting rules of safety
   b. following safety rules too closely
   c. trying to save money by ignoring safety

7. It appears to be a peculiar feature of our shared moral legacy that bad things seem to happen to <u>underprivileged people</u>, whether through negligence, conspiracy, or just plain bad luck.
   a. people who are not paid minimum wage
   b. people who are in the wrong place at the wrong time
   c. people with a lower standard of living or fewer rights

8. Who knows where the underground tanks of petroleum are located? Who knows if the whole station might suddenly <u>ignite</u>?
   a. start to burn
   b. start to sink slowly
   c. disappear suddenly

9. Our silent response to <u>atrocities</u>, from the turn of the century to the dawning of the new millennium, <u>bears mute testimonial to</u> our lack of the moral virtue known as courage.
   a. fearful acts / clearly denies
   b. good acts / clearly announces
   c. wicked or cruel acts / is silent proof of

10 We don't lose sleep over the hole in the ozone, or the destruction of the rain forest, or how to <u>dispose of</u> nuclear waste because we know that someone is making everything all right.

   a. get rid of
   b. increase the amount of
   c. decrease the amount of

11 I recognize this attitude as a healthy <u>component of our survival instinct</u> and one that enables us to carry on so we can make additional choices that sustain us.

   a. part of our will to live
   b. part of the law of the world
   c. part of our need to take care of others

Follow-up Check and discuss your answers in pairs or with the class.

D Reading for overall meaning

Read the article at a quick but comfortable pace. Then answer this question:

Today, is the author comfortable with the decision his father made at the gas station years before?

A Gas Station Burns in the Forest: Illuminating Our Moral Legacy

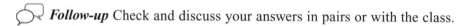

David A. Shapiro

About 300 yards outside the entrance to Glacier National Park in Montana are two gas stations, one on either side of the two-lane road. They have been strategically placed so tourists can fill up before entering the park and refill upon leaving. The one on the left is a national brand, the one on the right, a local Mom 'n Pop cut-price place called Y-Pay-Mor. We, of course, have chosen the national brand—quality, my dad likes to remind me, is worth a few pennies extra. Besides, the cut-rate places don't take credit cards, and gasoline, for convenience and accounting, is always purchased by credit card—that's just how it's done.

We have completed filling our vehicle's huge 32-gallon tank, have stocked up on peanuts and gum, and paid. With my father behind the wheel, me in the passenger seat, and my best friend lounging at the motor home's kitchen table, we are just beginning to pull out. It is almost dusk and we are in a hurry to find our reserved campsite before it gets dark.

continued

Just as my father angles the Winnebago onto the road, an explosion rocks the gas station across the street. Through the corner of my window, I see a fireball engulf its white clapboard office. I perceive the image of a man inside completely on fire, staggering toward what had been the door, and rolling on the ground, over and over. A woman comes running from the back, pointing at the right side of the building where the restrooms are. She waves her arms at the blazing structure and cries, "My baby! My baby is in there!"

By this time, we are on the road and pulling away. I look at my dad. "Did you see that?! Should we stop?"

He is fighting to disbelieve what he only half-saw. The expression on his face is one I've never seen before. His eyes are wide; they look simultaneously young and ancient, somehow. His jaw is clenched and his hands are tight around the steering wheel. He is slightly hunched over, as if urging our vehicle forward. He focuses on the road ahead, hits the brakes as a man in jeans and a T-shirt sprints across in front of us and toward the fire, then accelerates again.

"Dad! There was a guy, I think, on fire! Shouldn't we do something?"

My dad says that he didn't see any guy and even if there was, there's nothing we can do. It's too dangerous and there are other people already on the scene. It's better we should hurry up to the park entrance and tell the rangers.

When we get there, a small crowd has assembled and is looking back at the plume of black smoke that is now funneling upwards. One park ranger is inside the toll booth, talking hurriedly on the phone. A second stands outside with his arms folded, watching the smoke rise, looking bewildered. My father explains to him what has happened. The ranger gratefully acknowledges the information, tells us it will help, and says that we should move inside the park so emergency vehicles can get through.

We drive off toward our campground. I ask my father if we should go back after we get set up.

"We've done the best we could do," he says. "The right people have been informed. It's under control now."

That's the last we ever talk about it.

Did we do the right thing? What is the moral legacy of the choice we made? How does it mirror the moral legacy of our time? As I recall what happened and as I consider how our society will be remembered, I see many similarities between this microcosmic memory and the macrocosmic legacy we as a people will leave behind.

I begin by considering the setting, which strikes me as a particularly apt metaphor for this day and age—two gas stations outside a National Park. Note that one of the stations is a corporate franchise; it's a clean, well-lighted place. The other, unsupported by the conglomerate, is a dilapidated shanty. The former serves well-to-do customers, people who tour National Parks in Winnebagos, who pay by credit card, who think that a tidy bathroom and monthly statements of account are worth the extra cost. Customers at the latter pay by

continued

cash, they drive beat-up station wagons and camp outside, in tents or under the stars. To them, gas is gas—why pay more?

Tragedy strikes. Tragically, it strikes the less affluent station. Hasn't this been the trend throughout the 20th century, particularly when technology is involved? Bhopal, Chernobyl, the Marshall Islands—time and time again, less-developed places bear the brunt of the technology that sustains more developed ones.

Why did Y-Pay-Mor and not our station explode? Were its owners cutting corners on safety in order to keep up with their corporate-supported competitor across the street? Or were they simply not as well-informed as to the dangers? Perhaps they didn't have the resources—educational or financial—to guarantee a sufficient degree of safety. Or maybe they were just unlucky. Again, it appears to be a peculiar feature of our shared moral legacy that bad things seem to happen to underprivileged people, whether through negligence, conspiracy, or just plain bad luck.

Next, I see us driving away—in a motor home, no less—as a man burns and a mother screams for her child. Conceivably, we could have stopped and done something, but we didn't. I consider all the reasons that modern society doesn't stop and do something and the explanations seem identical.

First, we are afraid. Afraid for ourselves, of course, but even more, we are afraid for our loved ones, and most of all, for our children.

My father has his son next to him; his son's best friend—the child of his own dear friend, a youngster he has known since the boy was born—sits nearby, and across the street, not 50 yards away, a gas station office has exploded. He doesn't know why, or what might happen next. My father is a physician, not an engineer. Who knows where the underground tanks of petroleum are located? Who knows if the whole station might suddenly ignite? Maybe both stations share some sort of underground storage—the entire road could blow. At the very least, we are carrying 32 gallons of gasoline ourselves. We've got to get away, and get away quickly. We must remove ourselves and our families from any potential danger.

One doesn't have to sift carefully though the legacy of our time to see how fear has colored our moral choices. Our silent response to atrocities, from the turn of the century to the dawning of the new millennium, bears mute testimonial to our lack of the moral virtue known as courage.

Of course, we also don't know how we can help—if at all. We're too late, we don't have the skills, nothing can be done. My father says that if the man were on fire, no one could save him. We don't do anything because we think what we could do won't be enough. What difference will it make anyway?

As a society, we take this same moral stance. Our legacy is one of inaction—not simply through lack of compassion, but through lack of knowledge. We're paralyzed because we feel powerless. We're silent because we feel dumb. If no one can do anything, why should we?

Besides, we do what we can. We report the accident to the proper agency. We

continued

let those in charge take care of things. After all, that's what they're there for. We get out of the way so they can do their jobs. Those people are experts; they know what they're doing. If anyone's in trouble, they'll see to it that people are cared for.

Isn't this the code of behavior that most of us have accepted? We assume that the experts will solve our problems for us. We don't lose sleep—not too much, anyway—over the hole in the ozone, or the destruction of the rain forest, or how to dispose of nuclear waste, because we know that somewhere, somebody is making everything all right. We just have to let them know what's happening, and they'll figure it out. As a result, we can look back and know that—despite our inaction—we did our part, small as it was. But our descendants—if there are any—what will they think? Will they look at our failure to take personal action and assume that we didn't care?

But we do care. We just have to get on with our lives. It's getting dark. We still have many miles to go. We've never been here before. We're tired and hungry. How can we help anyone when we're in this state of mind? We've got to get our own act together before we can help others, don't we?

I know that many people nowadays—myself included—often feel this way. I recognize this attitude as a healthy component of our survival instinct and one that enables us to carry on so we can make additional choices—moral or not—that sustain us. But I wonder what our world would be like if this survival-first message was the moral legacy of Socrates or of Martin Luther King, Jr., or of Gandhi.

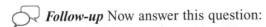 *Follow-up* Now answer this question:

Today, is the author comfortable with the decision his father made at the gas station years before?

E Reading for more detail

Read the article a second time. Use the questions to read for more detail and to bring your experience to the reading.

1 What can we conclude about the social and economic status of the author's family?

2 Which element of the explosion was the most frightening for you to read?

3 How do we know that the father was aware of the explosion? Can you think of a situation where you had the same nervous reaction as the father?

4 Would you have made the same decision as the father to drive on when the explosion occurred? Explain.

5 How did you answer the question at the end of *Notes on the Reading?* Were you right?

6 What two major reasons does the author give for not stopping to help in the tragedy? Which one seems like a better reason to you?

7 Does the author's explanation of their inaction seem like a logical analysis or just a rationalization to you? Explain.

8 What world problems do we leave to the experts? To what extent do you agree with this attitude? Explain.

9 *Key words* Make a list of six words and expressions that you feel are important to the reading. Be ready to explain what each word means and why it is important.

Follow-up Discuss your answers in pairs, in small groups, or as a class.

PART 2
PERSONAL WRITTEN RESPONSE

Ⓐ Journals: A private audience

Choose two of the following topics. Write for about 20 minutes in your journal notebook. These journal entries are for your eyes only, so do not spend a lot of time using a dictionary or worrying about grammar.

1. What is your opinion of the father in the anecdote? Of the son?
2. Are people in affluent modern countries less likely than people from less developed countries to help others in a tragedy?
3. Do you agree with the author that less developed places bear the brunt of the technology that sustains more developed places? Explain.
4. In your opinion, are people in general indifferent to the suffering of others?

Ⓑ Shared writing

Choose two of the following topics, and write for a total of 20 minutes. Your audience is your classmates, with whom you will share your writing. They will be interested not only in what you feel but also in why you feel that way. Express your views clearly and support them.

1. Have you witnessed a tragedy similar to the one we read about? If so, describe the incident and what other people did—or didn't do.
2. Describe an incident where you had to decide whether to stop and help or to get on with your life. Why did you decide as you did? How do you feel about your decision?
3. Do you agree with the author that most of us often take a similar moral stance in a tragedy: We choose inaction through lack of compassion and lack of knowledge?
4. Do we have a moral duty to help others even if helping them threatens our safety or the safety of loved ones?

Ⓒ Feedback on your writing

Get feedback on how clear and logical your thinking and writing are. Select one of the questions from *Shared Writing,* and read your answer to a small group of classmates. Follow the *Peer Feedback Guidelines* on page 11.

PART 3

FURTHER READING, WRITING, AND DISCUSSION

- What is Dr. Martin Luther King, Jr., known for?
- Why is this demonstration taking place?

A Preparing to read

INTRODUCTION

The excerpt which follows is from a speech entitled "The Trumpet of Conscience," delivered by Dr. Martin Luther King, Jr., in 1967. Dr. King was a famous U.S. civil rights leader and Christian preacher. He worked for the rights of the poor and of African Americans and other minorities. Dr. King was waging a war against poverty and discrimination while the U.S. government was waging a war against North Vietnam. The United States was fighting the Communist forces of North Vietnam and supporting the National Liberation Front of South Vietnam. Dr. King spoke out against violence as a way to solve problems and achieve civil rights goals. His support of non-violence was in sharp contrast to the violence of the war in Vietnam. In his speech "The Trumpet of Conscience," Dr. King expresses his opposition to the Vietnam War. We learn that Dr. King's decision to oppose the war was not an easy one when he tells us he was confused and *perplexed* by the *complexities* and *ambiguities* of the war. He knew that neither side, North Vietnam or the National Liberation Front, was a *paragon of virtue*, a model of just and good behavior. As a preacher, he also knew that conflicts can only be resolved when there is *give-and-take* from both sides.

(*Note:* Words in italics are from the reading.)

It is many months now since I found myself obliged by conscience to end my silence and to take a public stand against my country's war in Vietnam. The considerations which led me to that painful decision have not disappeared; indeed, they have been magnified by the course of events since then. The war itself is intensified; the impact on my country is even more destructive. I cannot speak about the great themes of violence and non-violence, of social change and of hope for the future, without reflecting on the tremendous violence of Vietnam. Since the Spring of 1967, when I first made public my opposition to my government's policy, many persons have questioned me about the wisdom of my decision. "Why you?" they have said. "Peace and civil rights don't mix. Aren't you hurting the cause of your people?" And when I hear such questions, I have been greatly saddened, for they mean that the inquirers have never really known me, my commitment, or my calling. Indeed, that question suggests that they do not know the world in which they live.

In explaining my position, I have tried to make it clear that I remain perplexed—as I think everyone must be—by the complexities and ambiguities of Vietnam. I would not wish to underrate the need for a collective solution to this tragic war. I would wish neither to present North Vietnam or the National Liberation Front as paragons of virtue nor to overlook the role they can play in the successful resolution of the problem. While they both may have justifiable reasons to be suspicious of the good faith of the United States, life and history give eloquent testimony to the fact that conflicts are never resolved without trustful give-and-take on both sides. Since I am a preacher by calling, I suppose it is not surprising that I had several reasons for bringing Vietnam into the field of my moral vision. There is at the outset a very obvious and almost facile connection between the war in Vietnam and the struggle I and others have been waging in America.

REFLECTION AND DISCUSSION

Answer the following questions about the excerpt.

1 Why did Dr. King feel that he had to clarify his position against the war?

2 Why didn't Dr. King feel the United States could solve the problems between the two sides in Vietnam by fighting there?

3 Why did Dr. King bring Vietnam into the field of his moral vision? In other words, how did his concern for poor Americans grow into a concern for the people in Vietnam?

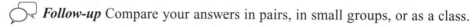 *Follow-up* Compare your answers in pairs, in small groups, or as a class.

NOTES ON THE READING

In the remainder of the speech, King gives us three reasons that he sees a connection between the war in Vietnam and his war on poverty in the United States. First, the U.S. government had been making efforts to help poor Americans through poverty programs that provided assistance in education, nutrition, and employment. However, the entry of the United States into war had eviscerated* these programs because all the money, men, and skills were eaten up by the war, which was like an evil, destructive force. Second, besides devastating the hopes of African Americans at home, the country sent them to fight and die in higher proportions than other Americans. Young men who were neglected by their own society were sent thousands of miles to guarantee others rights they themselves didn't have. Third, King told young people in U.S. ghettos that Molotov cocktails (homemade bombs) and rifles would never solve their problems at home, that a solution could only come through nonviolence. Could Dr. King speak out against violence in the ghetto without speaking out against a bigger purveyor* of violence, his own government, in Vietnam? Dr. King knew segregated accommodations* were wrong. How could he segregate his moral concern by not including the Vietnamese people?

eviscerated: *taken out the internal supports*
purveyor: *supplier, source*
segregated accomodations: *separation of blacks and whites with different rights, services, and freedoms*

(*Note:* When this speech was given, the accepted term for Americans of African heritage was Blacks. Now the accepted term is African Americans.)

B Reading for overall meaning

Finish reading the selection to answer this question:

Was Dr. King as concerned about Vietnamese victims of the war as he was about U.S. victims? Explain.

The Trumpet of Conscience

Rev. Dr. Martin Luther King, Jr.

A few years ago there was a shining moment in that struggle. It seemed as if there was a real promise of hope for the poor, both black and white, through the poverty program. There were experiments, hopes, new beginnings. Then came the buildup in Vietnam, and I watched the program broken and eviscerated as if it were some idle political plaything of a society gone mad on war, and I knew that America would never invest the necessary funds or energies in rehabilitation of its poor so long as adventures like Vietnam continued to draw men and skills and money like some demoniacal destructive suction tube. And so I was increasingly compelled to see the war not only as a moral outrage but also as an enemy of the poor, and to attack it as such.

Perhaps a more tragic recognition of reality took place when it became clear to me that the war was doing far more than devastating the hopes of the poor at home. It was sending their sons and their brothers and their husbands to fight and die in extraordinarily higher proportions relative to the rest of the population. We were taking the Black young men who had been crippled by our society and sending them eight thousand miles away to guarantee liberties in Southeast Asia which they had not found in southwest Georgia and east Harlem. And so we have been repeatedly faced with the cruel irony of watching Negro and white boys on the TV screen as they kill and die together for a nation that has been unable to seat them together in the same schools. We watch them in brutal solidarity burning the huts of a poor village, but we realize that they would never live on the same block in Detroit. I could not be silent in the face of such cruel manipulation of the poor.

My third reason moves to even deeper level of awareness, but it grows out of my experience in the ghettos of the North over the last three years—especially the last three summers. As I walked among the desperate, rejected, angry young men, I have told them that Molotov cocktails and rifles would not solve their problems. I have tried to offer them my deepest compassion, while maintaining my conviction that social change comes most meaningfully through nonviolent action. But, they asked, and rightly so, what about Vietnam? They asked if our own nation wasn't using massive doses of violence to solve its problems, to bring about the changes it wanted. Their questions hit home, and I knew that I could never again raise my voice against the violence of the oppressed in the ghettos without first having spoken clearly to the greatest purveyor of violence in the world today: my own government. For the sake of those boys, for the sake of this government, for the sake of the hundreds of thousands trembling under our violence, I cannot be silent. For those who ask the question, "Aren't you a civil rights leader?"—and thereby mean to exclude me from the movement for peace—I answer that I have worked too long and hard now

continued

> against segregated accommodations to end up segregating my moral concern. Justice is indivisible. It must also be said that it would be rather absurd to work passionately and unrelentingly for integrated schools and not be concerned with the survival of a world in which to be integrated.
>
> To me the relationship of this [Christian ministry] to the making of peace is so obvious that I sometimes marvel at those who ask me why I am speaking against the war. We [clergy] are called to speak for the weak, for the voiceless, for the victims of our nation, and for those it calls enemy, for no document from human hands can make these humans any less our brothers.

Follow-up Now answer this question:

Was Dr. King as concerned about Vietnamese victims of the war as he was about U.S. victims? Explain.

C Reading for more detail

Read the selection again. Mark any places in the text that are still unclear to you.

D Helping each other understand

Write for 20 minutes on this selection. Write about one or more of the following questions:

1 What do you have trouble understanding?

2 Do you think disputes between countries can be solved without violence?

3 What point or opinion in the speech do you agree or disagree with strongly?

Follow-up Read what you have written to a small group of students. Read your reaction a second time if necessary. Each group member will respond with (1) a question, (2) a comment, and/or (3) help with what you didn't understand.

E Discussion: Critical thinking

Discuss these questions in pairs, in small groups, or as a class.

1 What did Dr. King mean when he said, "Justice is indivisible"?

2 Life has many rules—some from religion, many from government, and others from society. Does obeying all the rules make a person moral? Explain.

3 When a government starts a war, its position is that it is acting justly and morally. If a citizen refuses to participate in the war because of personal moral principles, is he/she less moral than the government? Explain.

PART 4

FOCUS ON WRITING SKILLS

Ⓐ Using another's writing: Summarizing a passage

In the opening passage of "A Gas Station Burns in the Forest," Shapiro describes an incident that might be useful to you in your formal writing assignment. However, you will want to tell what happened in a few words, in a summary. The author uses the present tense to add drama to the event and to make it seem as if we were at the scene of the accident with him. In your summary use the past tense (simple and past progressive), and give the essence of the passage, not every detail. It is usually a good idea to do a first draft, which you later revise for accuracy and conciseness.

EXERCISE 1 *Summarizing the explosion incident*

Reread lines 1–45 of the story. Then write a summary of the incident, using the opening statement given below. Add three to five general sentences to support that statement. Limit yourself to one paragraph of 100 words, including this first sentence.

When Shapiro remembers the explosion he saw while on a trip with his father and a friend, he has doubts about the morality of their reaction.

💬 ***Follow-up*** Exchange and discuss summaries with another student. Did you include the same essential points of the story?

Ⓑ Meeting reader expectations: Persuasive essays

In Chapter 3 we discussed the informative and persuasive nature of academic writing (page 73). In Chapters 3, 4, and 5, you wrote informative essays intended to prove a logical assertion that you formulated in a thesis statement.

Persuasive essays are different from informative essays because in a persuasive essay the writer expresses an opinion on a controversial issue and argues convincingly in support of that opinion. For example, the issue might be whether being against war is unpatriotic or whether people are by nature good or bad.

To support your position in a persuasive essay, remember that people seldom accept others' opinions just as they are. An intelligent listener or reader wants evidence that supports an opinion. Do not limit yourself to your own logical arguments—there are many forms of persuasive support. Some examples are listed below.

1 *Expert opinion* The ideas of an author or someone else who is recognized as knowing a lot about your topic can be good support. Make sure you agree with the expert.

2. *Facts, statistics* Facts may not be more interesting than opinions, but they are more convincing. You will have to do research to present useful, accurate facts. Do not make up your own statistics. Look for facts at the library or do a search on the Internet.

3. *Examples* Real examples, that is, ones from your own experience, are better support than hypothetical ones from your imagination.

4. *Personal anecdote* This is a short narrative. A personal anecdote can be a very effective argument if it supports the main idea closely.

5. *Description* A well-written description that appeals to the senses (sight, hearing, touch, smell, taste) is effective if the description is relevant to the point of the essay.

EXERCISE 2 *Teacher persuasive essay*

Read this essay a first time to see if you agree with the writer's position on patriotism. Read it a second time to answer the questions that follow it.

Patriotic—and Against War

Reading Dr. Martin Luther King's essay about the Vietnam War reminded me of an antiwar demonstration that I participated in some time ago. I went because it seemed my country was going to war, and I didn't understand why. In the news coverage of the other demonstrations, I noticed with some surprise that many people—government officials, Hollywood celebrities, journalists, and even some veterans of other wars—occasionally called antiwar protestors unpatriotic. By unpatriotic, I suppose they thought that protestors did not love their country. However, I felt it was a very patriotic gesture to take a stand against war. To know that I can be both patriotic *and* against war, I need only think carefully about the definition of patriotism, consider what my religion tells me about war, and look at the economic and human losses that war has brought to the world.

A quick look at the dictionary might make a person mistakenly think that a war protestor is unpatriotic. The dictionary explains that patriotism is a love of one's country and a willingness to defend it. If we love our country, it seems logical that we should want what is best for the country and her people. For me, that means my country will deal honestly and fairly with other countries and responsively and compassionately with her citizens. Am I ready to defend my country? If we were attacked, I am sure I would make every effort to do what was needed to help those in need. Would I support a war in a country thousands of miles away because of a suspicion that that country could harm the United States? No, a suspicion should not guide how a country conducts foreign affairs. In addition, attacking another country because of a suspicion

continued

goes against the teachings of many wise nonviolent leaders like Mohandas Gandhi and Martin Luther King, Jr. It is also against the principles of the religion that I follow.

People of my religion believe that God exists in all people. Since we believe that God is in each person, it follows that we cannot consider anyone an enemy. Therefore, people of my religion are pacifists—against all war. Being against all war brings with it a very big obligation: to work for justice in the world in order to remove the reason for war. Peace and justice are, therefore, inseparable. This commitment to peace and justice has sometimes led people of my religion to civil disobedience (for example, a nonviolent demonstration). At other times, they have become conscientious objectors. Thomas Jefferson, one of the founding fathers of the United States, felt that the constitutional freedom of religion was an American's most sacred right. In following the principles of my religion, I am exercising a right guaranteed by the Constitution. Can it be unpatriotic to follow the Constitution? Can it be unpatriotic to want my country to interact with other countries in a spirit of peace and justice? My religion tells me neither action is unpatriotic.

Over 200 years ago, Thomas Jefferson said that the most successful war seldom pays for its losses. I assume that he was referring to the loss of human life, a loss far greater than the loss of land or weapons or political influence. In recent wars around the world, both sides have been weakened and impoverished. For example, the wars in Congo and Rwanda have devastated populations that were already among the world's poorest. War in the Middle East has left many people without adequate food, water, health care, work, and security. Even a rich country like the United States has domestic social needs that are neglected when a vast part of the nation's budget goes to paying for war. When 50 million people have no health care, when many children receive an inferior education because they live in poor neighborhoods, and when many peoples' lives are so hopeless that they look to drugs as a solution—I have to conclude that it is immoral for the government to spend billions of dollars on war. We can't even begin to put a value on the lives of soldiers and civilians who have died in wars.

If patriotism means a love of one's country, I have to question the patriotism of any government which endangers the lives of its soldiers in a war. If patriotism also means a willingness to defend one's country, then it is unwise for a government to make decisions that make the world less safe and the country itself in greater need of defense. Is it unpatriotic of me to be against war and to question my government's right to wage war? My understanding of patriotism, my religion, and the huge losses of war all tell me that it is clearly not unpatriotic to be against war. Furthermore, I am confident Thomas Jefferson, Mohandas Gandhi, and Martin Luther King, Jr., would all support my position.

1. Does the writer give enough information in the introduction for you to understand his position?

2. Which sentence states the writer's thesis? Do you agree with the writer's position on patriotism?

3. How many body paragraphs support the thesis? Which body paragraph is the most persuasive in your opinion? The least persuasive? Explain.

4. What does the writer's voice tell us about the writer?

5. Overall, do you find the essay persuasive? What would you change if you wrote an essay on the same topic?

C Sentence grammar: Consistency in tense, person, number, and tone

CONSISTENCY IN TENSE

Shifts in verb tense should only be done when necessary and logically consistent. If there is an error in verb tense, the text will not be clear to the reader. In this example, the writer is remembering in the present something that happened in the past.

I *remember* that he *put on* the parking brake before he *turned off* the engine.

A logically inconsistent shift in tense, however, is confusing to the reader:

WRONG a. I *cleaned* the ice from the window while the car *is running*.

    b. He *thought* his sister *was* busy and *cannot see* him.

Since all the verbs in the two examples above describe actions in the past, they should all be in the past tense.

CORRECT a. I *cleaned* the ice from the windshield while the car *was running*.

    b. He *thought* his sister *was* busy and *could not see* him.

EXERCISE 3 *Correcting for consistency in tense*

Read the passage below. Decide which verbs are not logical or consistent in tense, and correct them.

Our teacher let us out of class early so that we can go to a lecture on campus one day last week. The lecture began late, so we have to wait. I am usually impatient, so I become upset when we had to wait 15 minutes for the talk to begin. Since I know a lot about geology, I was able to follow the lecture, but many of my classmates can't. I noticed that one of my classmates, Mario, is sleeping. Fortunately, our teacher isn't there because I think she would have been angry with him.

CONSISTENCY IN PERSON AND NUMBER

Ideas and events can be expressed from different perspectives: first, second, or third person, singular or plural. Compare the following examples:

   a. *Students* need to find a quiet place to think and write if *they* want produce high quality work. (third person plural)

   b. *We* need to find a quiet place to think and write if *we* want to produce high quality work. (first person plural)

   c. *You* need find a quiet place to think and write if *you* want to produce high quality work. (second person)

Once you have chosen a perspective from which to express an idea, it is important to avoid unnecessary and illogical shifts in person and number. An unnecessary or illogical shift in person or number is confusing to readers, as in these examples:

WRONG   a. *One* has to be careful when *you* buy a used car.

(There's a shift from third person to second person for no reason.)

WRONG   b. *We* often buy clothes on sale because *I* can save a lot of money that way.

(There's a shift from plural to singular first person that is not called for by the context.)

In these revised examples, the inconsistencies in person and number have been corrected:

CORRECT   a. *You* have to be careful when *you* buy a used car. (informal)

—or—

One has to be careful when *one* buys a new car. (formal)

   b. *I* often buy clothes on sale because *I* can save a lot of money that way.

—or—

We often buy clothes on sale because *we* can save a lot of money that way.

EXERCISE 4 *Correcting for consistency in person and number*

Rewrite the sentences, correcting the shifts in person and number. You may need to change verbs and possessive pronouns to agree with new subjects.

1 Anyone can learn a foreign language if you study.

2 Everyone has the ability to learn, so students should never give up when it seems difficult to us.

3 We also need to keep in mind that one might be better at oral skills than at reading and writing, and vice versa.

4 Students should be proud of their strengths but at the same time be willing to work on your weaknesses.

5 Students often focus on vocabulary, but you need to realize that vocabulary is only one part of a language.

6 A language learner should remember that they can't communicate without knowing the structure and phonology of a language.

THE INFORMAL *YOU*

In conversation when you say *you*, it is obvious because of context whom you are referring to. For example, if your roommate at school said this to you,

"I suggest you register for classes early to avoid waiting in line,"

it would be clear whom your roommate was referring to.

In formal writing, however, the context in which your writing will be interpreted and who your audience will be is unknown. Therefore, it might not be clear whom *you* refers to, and it is best to avoid it. In addition, addressing your audience with *you* in a piece of writing lends it a friendly conversational tone that is not appropriate in academic writing. Using the third person is more precise and more formal. Compare the examples below.

INFORMAL   a. You need to heat the solution 120 degrees Celsius.

b. *You* could see how much pain the patient was in.

c. If *you* live in Miami, *you* must have air-conditioning.

FORMAL   a. The solution needs to be heated to 120 degrees Celsius.

b. *It* was evident how much pain the patient was in.

—or—

A person could see how much pain the patient was in.

c. To live in Miami, *one* must have air-conditioning.

EXERCISE 5 *Avoiding the informal* you

Rewrite these sentences, deleting or replacing *you* to produce more precise, formal sentences. Make any other necessary changes as well.

1 During the afternoon, when it's very hot in my country, you need to dress in cooler clothes.

2 You should try to avoid wearing dark colors.

3 You can't wear shorts in public in my country, however.

4 People consider wearing shorts indecent, so shorts aren't suitable for you to wear.

5 At home, of course, you can wear whatever you want.

6 If you receive company, though, you should make sure you look presentable.

CONSISTENCY IN TONE

It is important to maintain a consistent formal tone in academic writing, and to avoid the use of informal or colloquial language. Notice the shifts from informal to formal tone in the following examples.

INFORMAL   a. The university president addressed the faculty at length on issues including tenure, salary, the importance of research, and *hanging out with students*.

b. The faculty reported that raises of less than a thousand *bucks* per year would be unacceptable.

FORMAL   a. The university president addressed the faculty at length on issues including tenure, salary, the importance of research, and *faculty-student relationships*.

b. The faculty reported that raises of less than a thousand *dollars* per year would be unacceptable.

EXERCISE 6 *Correcting for consistency in tone*

Change the words and expressions in italics to maintain a formal tone.

1 John *blew off* his math class to prepare for his history exam.

2 It was difficult to give the accident victim the necessary medical attention because he was *screaming his head off*.

3 Two *guys* approached the managing editor's office to see what the excitement was *all about*.

4 A family with many *kids* will find making ends meet more difficult.

5 Marcella remarked that John's new sunglasses were *pretty cool*.

6 Smaller children often refuse to eat vegetables, which they find *yucky*.

7 Archie will probably have trouble selling his car for a good price because it is *a piece of junk*.

8 The students reported that they had had an *awesome* time on their spring vacation.

EXERCISE 7 *Editing for consistency in tense, person, number, and tone*

Read the paragraph below, underlining any shifts in tense, person, number, and tone. Then rewrite the paragraph, correcting the shifts.

The issue of doing what is right can be a difficult one for a foreign student. Sometimes the difference in how two cultures viewed things was extreme. It can even drive you nuts. I remember once my instructor asked to see me in her office later that afternoon. I agreed to see her at 3:00, but then my sister calls me on my cell phone from her car. She says she has a flat tire and is waiting on the side of the highway. Of course, I went to help her out. In the next class with the professor, she was very aggressive and asked why I don't keep my appointment. I guess I should have called her, but in the urgency of my sister's call, I forget to. My professor was real mad. To this day, she treats me like a liar—she doubted every word I say now. How are you supposed to act in a culture where a silly appointment is more important than my family?

PART 5
FORMAL WRITING ASSIGNMENT

A Writing topics

Read the topics, and choose one for your persuasive essay.

1. Is it unpatriotic for a person to be against war when his or her country is at war?
2. Is it easy to know the difference between right and wrong in life?
3. Are people by nature good and moral?

B Generating ideas: Panel discussion

Follow these steps to conduct a panel discussion on one of the writing topics.

1. Form two panels (groups) of two or three students each. One panel will answer "yes" to the chosen topic question and one will answer "no."
2. Using the board or a large sheet of paper, make two columns labeled *yes* and *no*. Each panel will write three to five one-sentence arguments supporting its position on the appropriate side of the board.
3. The panels will have five minutes each to discuss how they will refute the arguments (explain why they are wrong) on the opposing side.
4. The "yes" panel will attempt to refute the first point on the "no" list.
5. The "no" panel will attempt to refute the first point on the "yes" list.
6. The two panels take turns discussing points until all points have been addressed.

Follow-up Students in the audience may vote to decide which panel did the best job of defending its position and refuting the other side's points. After the panel discussion, all students should spend a few minutes taking notes on arguments they might use in their persuasive essays.

C Expanding your point of view: Research

To strengthen the arguments in your persuasive essay, you will probably want to use facts and possibly an expert opinion to support your position. The readings in this chapter may provide the support you need. If not, the best sources for facts and expert opinion are the Internet and the library.

When doing research, remember to write down bibliographical information for every source you might use in your essay. Include titles, authors, publishers, page numbers, Web page addresses, and so on. Take notes by paraphrasing or summarizing points that you can use in your essay.

D Initial drafts

FIRST DRAFT

Follow these steps when writing your first draft:

1. Start your first draft with an introduction that catches the interest of your readers and leads naturally to your thesis statement. Your thesis statement should reflect your position on the issue you have chosen.

2. Choose support for your position carefully. Remember that your opinion by itself is not persuasive. To be persuasive, your opinion must be backed up by facts, expert opinion, real examples, or relevant description and narrative.

3. If you need to think about your topic and position more, write freely for 15 or 20 minutes. Then read what you have written, and find at least three good main points for your support paragraphs. Continue free-writing if it helps you think.

4. If you already have enough ideas, outline your paper before writing the first draft to organize your ideas in a logical manner. (See Chapter 5, Part 4, Outlining, page 126.)

REVISION

Ask someone outside your class to read your first draft. Then ask the reader to summarize your position and argument to make sure these are understood. Find out what questions remain in the reader's mind after reading your draft.

With your reader's reaction in mind, evaluate your paper using the criteria listed in the *Essay Assessment Checklist* on page 164. Revise your first draft, and mark it "Draft 2."

E Review, revision, and assessment

PEER FEEDBACK

Read a classmate's paper, and give feedback using the *Essay Assessment Checklist* on page 164. Write your comments on the checklist, but make no marks on your classmate's paper. Give the checklist and the paper back to the writer. Answer any questions your classmate has about your feedback.

FURTHER REVISION

What did you learn from the feedback you received? Is your essay successful—is it convincing, interesting, clearly organized, and complete? If not, how can you make it more successful?

Revise your paper using the feedback you got in class. Give your teacher all drafts (with the last draft marked "Final draft") and the *Essay Assessment Checklist* completed by your classmate.

Writer's name: _____

Reader's name: _____

Essay Assessment Checklist   *Chapter 6*

These are the criteria for a well-written essay. Use them to examine your writing, or a classmate's, and check *Yes* or *No* for each item. You may wish to add comments or suggestions.

Content and ideas

	Yes	No	Reader's comments
1 The writer has thought carefully about the topic and supports the main points with enough evidence to persuade the reader of his or her position.	❏	❏	
2 The writer's voice is clear because he or she writes in a sincere way and keeps the audience in mind.	❏	❏	
3 The reader wants to continue reading to the end. It's interesting.	❏	❏	

Organization and form

4 The paper has a clear beginning, middle, and end. There are separate introductory, body, and concluding paragraphs.	❏	❏	
5 The essay moves logically in a straight line. The reader understands the writer's position and the support fully after one reading.	❏	❏	

Language

6 The paper is easy to understand. These elements are used well:			
• sentence structure	❏	❏	
• grammar			
• vocabulary	❏	❏	
• mechanics (spelling, capitalization, punctuation)	❏	❏	
• cohesive devices	❏	❏	
• consistency in tense, person, number, and tone	❏	❏	

CHAPTER 7

Progress and Tradition

- How are these two family meals different?
- Which family would you rather eat with? Why?

PART 1

INTRODUCTION TO THE TOPIC, READING, AND DISCUSSION

A Reflection

All of the following statements can apply to people from any country, whether very developed and rich or less developed and poor. But we often associate certain characteristics with certain levels of development in a country. Read each statement. Does it make you think of a rich, developed country? A poorer, less developed country? Both? Mark the blank *R* (rich), *P* (poor), or *R/P* (both).

_____ 1 People don't seem satisfied with their lives.

_____ 2 People depend a lot on their neighbors and relatives.

_____ 3 Violence, drug addiction, divorce, and suicide are not common problems in society.

_____ 4 Old people often seem to have no one to talk to but their pets.

_____ 5 People seem obsessed with* material things.

_____ 6 People tend to have emotional and mental problems rather than physical ones.

_____ 7 There is a strong sense of community and high level of cooperation among people when there's work to be done.

_____ 8 There is confusion about what constitutes morality.

_____ 9 There is a high level of frustration and depression among people.

_____ 10 People seem content with their lives.

obsessed with: *that is almost all they think about*

B Discussion

Discuss your answers above in pairs, small groups, or as a class.

C Preparing to read

NOTES ON THE READING

The Dalai Lama, the Buddhist spiritual leader of Tibet, has spent most of his life in exile outside his country. His position as an important spiritual leader and his life experiences have made him a popular author and commentator on religion and society. In his travels he comes into contact with many people from different backgrounds and different countries. In this selection he writes about his impressions of Western society and his ideas on how people can improve their lives. He contrasts the West with less developed societies to make his points clearer.

PREVIEWING THE VOCABULARY

Before reading, preview the vocabulary in context. Read these key sentences based on the text, and choose the best meanings for the underlined words.

1 My formative years were spent largely <u>cut off from</u> the realities of the twentieth century. This reflects the fact that we Tibetans had chosen—mistakenly, in my view—to remain <u>isolated</u> behind the high mountain ranges which separate our country from the rest of the world.
   a. in touch with / in contact with others
   b. unconcerned about / in a peaceful state
   c. out of touch with / having little contact with others

2 We all want to be happy. Everything we do, not only as individuals but also at the level of society, can be seen in terms of this <u>fundamental aspiration</u>.
   a. basic freedom
   b. basic way of breathing
   c. very important and strong desire

3 The desire to be happy and to avoid suffering knows no <u>boundaries</u>.
   a. limits
   b. reasons
   c. fulfillment

4 Everywhere, people are <u>striving</u> to improve their lives.
   a. too lazy
   b. forgetting
   c. trying hard

5 If we compare the rich with the poor, it often seems that those with nothing are, in fact, the least anxious, though they are <u>plagued with</u> physical pains and suffering.
   a. seldom bothered by
   b. continually troubled by
   c. concerned about the victims of

6 People in the West are so <u>caught up with</u> the idea of acquiring more things that they make no room for anything else in their lives.
   a. unaware of
   b. involved in
   c. unconcerned with

Progress and Tradition

7. They actually lose the dream of happiness. As a result, they are constantly tormented, torn between doubt about what might happen and the hope of gaining more.

   a. suffering
   b. comforted
   c. unable to decide

8. This paradox whereby inner suffering is so often found amid material wealth is so pervasive that we might wonder whether there is something in Western culture which predisposes people living there to such kinds of suffering.

   a. rare / protects people from
   b. difficult to find / makes people blind to
   c. common, found everywhere / creates a tendency for

9. The increasing autonomy that people enjoy as a result of advances in science and technology has its good points. In fact, it is possible today to be far more independent of others than ever before.

   a. dependence
   b. independence
   c. interdependence

10. In place of the sense of community and belonging, which is a common characteristic of less wealthy societies, we find a high degree of loneliness and alienation.

    a. feeling of independence
    b. feeling of belonging to the group
    c. feeling of separation from the group

Follow-up Check and discuss your answers in pairs or with the class.

D Reading for overall meaning

Read the selection at a quick but comfortable pace. Then answer this question:

According to the Dalai Lama, how have urbanization and advances in technology affected modern life?

Modern Society and the Quest for Human Happiness

The Dalai Lama

I am a comparative newcomer to the modern world. Although I fled my homeland as long ago as 1959, and although my life since then as a refugee in India has brought me into much closer contact with contemporary society, my formative years were spent largely cut off from the realities of the twentieth century. This was partly due to my appointment as Dalai Lama: I became a monk at a very early age. It also reflects the fact that we Tibetans had chosen—mistakenly, in my view—to remain isolated behind the high mountain ranges which separate our country from the rest of the world.

Today, however, I travel a great deal, and it is my good fortune continuously to be meeting new people. Moreover, individuals from all walks of life come to see me. Quite a lot—especially those who make the effort to travel to the Indian hill-station at Dharamsala where I live in exile—arrive seeking something. Among these are people who have suffered greatly: some have lost parents and children; some have friends or family who committed suicide; [some] are sick with cancer and with AIDS-related illnesses. Then, of course, there are fellow Tibetans with their own tales of hardship and suffering. Unfortunately, many have unrealistic expectations, supposing that I have healing powers or that I can give some sort of blessing. But I am only an ordinary human being. The best I can do is try to help them by sharing in their suffering.

For my part, meeting innumerable others from all over the world and from every walk of life reminds me of our basic sameness as human beings. Indeed, the more I see of the world, the clearer it becomes that no matter what our situation, whether we are rich or poor, educated or not, of one race, gender, religion, or another, we all desire to be happy and to avoid suffering. Our every intended action, in a sense our whole life—how we choose to live it within the context of the limitations imposed by our circumstances—can be seen as our answer to the great question which confronts us all: "How am I to be happy?"

We are sustained in this great quest for happiness, it seems to me, by hope. We know, even if we do not admit it, that there can be no guarantee of a better, happier life than the one we are leading today. As an old Tibetan proverb puts it, The next life or tomorrow—we can never be certain which will come first. But we hope to go on living. We hope that through this or that attraction we can bring about happiness. Everything we do, not only as individuals but also at the level of society, can be seen in terms of this fundamental aspiration. Indeed, it is one shared by all sentient beings. The desire or inclination to be happy and to avoid suffering knows no boundaries. It is in our nature. As such, it needs no justification and is validated by the simple fact that we naturally and correctly want this.

continued

And this is precisely what we see in countries both rich and poor. Everywhere, by all means imaginable, people are striving to improve their lives. Yet strangely, my impression is that those living in the materially developed countries, for all their industry, are in some ways less satisfied, are less happy, and suffer more than those living in the least developed countries. Indeed, if we compare the rich with the poor, it often seems that those with nothing are, in fact, the least anxious, though they are plagued with physical pains and suffering. As for the rich, while a few know how to use their wealth intelligently—that is to say, not in luxurious living but by sharing it with the needy—many do not. They are so caught up with the idea of acquiring still more that they make no room for anything else in their lives. In their absorption, they actually lose the dream of happiness, which riches were to have provided. As a result, they are constantly tormented, torn between doubt about what might happen and the hope of gaining more, and plagued with mental and emotional suffering—even though outwardly they may appear to be leading entirely successful and comfortable lives. This is suggested both by the high degree and by the disturbing prevalence among the populations of the materially developed countries of anxiety, discontent, frustration, uncertainty, and depression. Moreover, this inner suffering is clearly connected with growing confusion as to what constitutes morality and what its foundations are.

I am often reminded of this paradox when I go abroad. It frequently happens that when I arrive in a new country, at first everything seems very pleasant, very beautiful. Everybody I meet is very friendly. There is nothing to complain about. But then, day by day as I listen, I hear people's problems, their concerns, and worries. They experience feelings of isolation; then follows depression. The result is the troubled atmosphere which is such a feature of the developed world.

At first, this surprised me. Although I never imagined that material wealth alone could ever overcome suffering, looking at the developed world from Tibet, a country materially always very poor, I must admit that I thought wealth would have gone further toward reducing suffering than is actually the case. I expected that with physical hardship much reduced, as it is for the majority living in the industrially developed countries, happiness would be much easier to achieve than for those living under more severe conditions. Instead, the extraordinary advancements of science and technology seem to have achieved little more than numerical improvement. In many cases, progress has meant hardly anything more than greater numbers of opulent houses in more cities, with more cars driving between them. Certainly there has been a reduction in some types of suffering, including especially certain illnesses. But it seems to me that there has been no overall reduction.

Saying this, I remember well an occasion on one of my early trips to the West. I was the guest of a very wealthy family who lived in a large, well-appointed house. Everyone was very charming and polite. There were servants to cater to one's every need, and I began to think that here, perhaps, was proof

continued

positive that wealth could be a source of happiness. My hosts definitely had an air of relaxed confidence. But when I saw in the bathroom, through a cupboard door which was slightly open, an array of tranquilizers and sleeping pills, I was reminded forcefully that there is often a big gap between outward appearances and inner reality.

This paradox whereby inner—or we could say psychological and emotional—suffering is so often found amid material wealth is readily apparent throughout much of the West. Indeed, it is so pervasive that we might wonder whether there is something in Western culture which predisposes people living there to such kinds of suffering? This I doubt. So many factors are involved. Clearly, material development itself has a role to play. But we can also cite the increasing urbanization of modern society, where high concentrations of people live in close proximity to one another. In this context, consider that in place of our dependence on one another for support, today, wherever possible, we tend to rely on machines and services. Whereas formerly farmers would call in all their family members to help with the harvest, today they simply telephone a contractor. We find modern living organized so that it demands the least possible direct dependence on others. The more or less universal ambition seems to be for everyone to own their own house, their own car, their own computer, and so on in order to be as independent as possible. This is natural and understandable. We can also point to the increasing autonomy that people enjoy as a result of advances in science and technology. In fact, it is possible today to be far more independent of others than ever before. But with these developments, there has arisen a sense that my future is not dependent on my neighbor but rather on my job or, at most, my employer. This in turn encourages us to suppose that because others are not important for my happiness, their happiness is not important to me.

We have, in my view, created a society in which people find it harder and harder to show one another basic affection. In place of the sense of community and belonging, which we find such a reassuring feature of less wealthy (and generally rural) societies, we find a high degree of loneliness and alienation. Despite the fact that millions live in close proximity to one another, it seems that many people, especially among the old, have no one to talk to but their pets. Modern industrial society often strikes me as being like a huge self-propelled machine. Instead of human beings in charge, each individual is a tiny, insignificant component with no choice but to move when the machine moves.

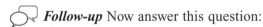 *Follow-up* Now answer this question:

> *According to the Dalai Lama, how have urbanization and advances in technology affected modern life?*

E Reading for more detail

Read the selection a second time. Use the questions to read for more detail and to bring your experience to the reading.

1. Does the Dalai Lama heal the people who come to him for help? Explain.
2. To what basic question does everyone seek an answer? Is this the basic question in your life?
3. How are people in rich countries and poor countries different in the Dalai Lama's opinion? Do you agree?
4. When he travels to a new place in the West, how do his impressions change over time?
5. What factors explain the suffering in the West, according to the Dalai Lama?
6. *Key words* Make a list of six key words and expressions that you feel are important to the reading. Be ready to explain what each word means and why it is important.

Follow-up Discuss your answers in pairs, in small groups, or as a class.

PART 2

PERSONAL WRITTEN RESPONSE

Ⓐ Journals: A private audience

Choose two of the following topics. Write for about 20 minutes in your journal notebook. These journal entries are for your eyes only, so do not spend a lot of time using a dictionary or worrying about grammar.

1 Did you like this reading? Explain.

2 Would you rather spend your life in a very developed country or in a less developed one? Explain.

3 If you could talk to the Dalai Lama, what would you say to him? What questions would you ask him? Why?

Ⓑ Shared writing

Choose two of the following topics, and write for a total of 20 minutes. Your audience is your classmates, with whom you will share your writing. They will be interested not only in what you feel but also in why you feel that way. Express your views clearly and support them.

1 Is the Dalai Lama's view of the world realistic? Explain.

2 Does being able to depend on other people only have advantages, or are there disadvantages, too? Explain.

3 If you have lived in both developed and less developed countries, what are the advantages of each?

4 The Dalai Lama implies that the problems he mentions (violence, drug addiction, divorce, suicide) are more serious than lack of material comforts. Do you agree?

Ⓒ Feedback on your writing

Get feedback on how clear and logical your thinking and writing are. Select one of the questions from *Shared Writing,* and read your answer to a small group of classmates. Follow the *Peer Feedback Guidelines* on page 11.

PART 3
FURTHER READING, WRITING, AND DISCUSSION

- What do these Chinese technicians appear to be doing?
- How might technological change affect life in China?
- Is new technology always beneficial to a country? Why or why not?

A Preparing to read

NOTES ON THE READING

Engineer, businessman, and adviser to the Indian government, Satyan Pitroda was born and educated in India. He did graduate studies in the United States, where he later worked on digital telephone switches. After much success, he turned his eye to his homeland, India, which he wanted to help by improving telephone service. Although cell phones are a common feature in India's large cities, the majority of Indians live in rural villages, the vast part of the country outside of the urban areas. In this article, Pitroda discusses the role of technology in developing countries of the Third World. He gives us his view of *appropriate technology,* technology which is suitable for the level of development of a country. In rural India, two examples of appropriate technology would be the *water screw,* a simple device to move water from a river to irrigate a field, and the *inclined plane,* a cable railroad to help trains climb steep mountain slopes.

(*Note:* Words in italics are from the reading.)

REFLECTION AND DISCUSSION

Before you read, think about your position on the use of technology in developing countries. Read each statement. If you agree, write *A;* if you disagree, write *D.*

_____ 1 Rich countries should help poor countries by making sure the uneducated rural poor get technology appropriate to their needs. (Appropriate technology would include immunization against disease, wells that provide clean water, electricity, and better sanitation.)

_____ 2 Higher technology like advanced telecommunications (for example, Internet connections and cell phones) is not appropriate for the developing nations. In other words, it is right not to provide "high-tech" assistance (state-of-the-art technology) in "low-tech" areas (poor rural areas).

_____ 3 Bringing information technology to poor people such as subsistence farmers (those who can only grow enough to feed themselves) is neither effective nor logical.

_____ 4 Increasing citizens' access to information through better telecommunications can be a democratizing force in that information is no longer controlled by a few people—it is available to every citizen.

_____ 5 Information technology can be a social leveler. That is, it can make different parts of the population more equal by destroying social barriers, correcting economic inequalities, and balancing intellectual disparities.

Follow-up Discuss your responses in pairs, in small groups, or as a class.

B Reading for overall meaning

Read the article the first time to answer this question:

Does the author appreciate technology more for its technical benefits or its social implications?

Development, Democracy, and the Village Telephone

Sam (Satyan) Pitroda

I was born in 1942 and raised in a poor village in one of the poorest areas of rural India, a place with kerosene lamps and no running water. In 1980, at 38, I was a U.S. citizen and a self-made telecommunications millionaire. By 1990, I was 47 years old and nearing the end of nearly a decade back in India. I was a leader of a controversial but largely successful effort to build an Indian information industry and begin the immense task of extending digital telecommunications to every corner of my native country, even to villages like the one where I was born.

The effort persists today at an increased pace, but it remains controversial. Some of the controversy has centered on me and my methods. Most of it focuses on the effectiveness and logic of bringing information technology to people who are in global terms the poorest of the poor.

Common sense and accepted thinking about economic development have long held it ridiculous to supply Third-World villages with state-of-the-art technology. What subsistence farmers need is not high-tech science and complex systems, the argument goes, but immunizations, basic literacy, disease- and drought-resistant cereals and oilseeds, simple pumps, deep-drop toilets, electricity—all the "appropriate" technologies that the unsophisticated rural poor can use and understand.

I agree with this argument as far as it goes. Third-World farming villages need water, hygiene, health, and power, and the need is usually great. But the argument falls short in its definition of "appropriate." It ignores technology's profound social implications. And it comes dangerously close to sentencing the Third-World poor to a life of third-rate capacities and opportunity.

For me, three facts about Third-World development stand out with great force. First, high technology is already an essential element in effective water sourcing, sanitation, construction, agriculture, and other development activities. Water surveys are carried out from satellites. Bioengineering has revolutionized crop production. Appropriate technology has moved well beyond the water screw and the inclined plane.

Second, modern telecommunications and electronic information systems are thoroughly appropriate technologies even in those regions of the world that still lack adequate water, food, and power. The reason is simply that modern telecommunications is an indispensable aid in meeting basic needs. If a U.S. community needed, say, widespread immunization or replacement of a power grid, would the telephone seem a vital or an irrelevant tool in getting the job done? Would the telephone seem more or less critical if the job were tied to a flood or drought and required the mobilization of resources over a broad area?

continued

Third, as a great social leveler, information technology ranks second only to death. It can destroy cultural barriers, overwhelm economic inequalities, even compensate for intellectual differences. In short, high technology can put unequal human beings on an equal footing, and that makes it the most potent democratizing tool ever devised. . . .

[Here Pitroda describes his work in India in detail, including: the creation of the Centre for Development of Telematics, or C-DOT; the installation of digital phone equipment partly manufactured in India; the installation of new telephone lines; and other improvements to the rural telephone system.]

C-DOT ran a test in Karnataka state with hugely encouraging results. In one town of 5,000 people with almost no previous telephone service, business activity rose many times following installation of an automatic digital exchange for 100 lines. Suddenly, it was possible for a truck owner to chase his drivers, line up goods and labor by telephone, and monitor the movement of his vehicles. Local farmers could call nearby cities and get real prices for their produce. Artisans could speak to customers, machine operators could arrange for service and repairs, shopkeepers could order goods—all by phone and in real time. In the six months after the introduction of service, total bank deposits in the town rose by an impressive 80 percent.

There were also social benefits. The townspeople could call doctors and ambulances, order pumps and textbooks, call newspapers, speak to politicians, share experiences with colleagues, and organize community ceremonies and functions. One villager told me that when his father died seven years earlier, he'd had to send 20 messengers on trains and buses to inform relatives in nearby villages. More recently when his mother followed, the villager went to the local tea shop and phoned all 20 villages—instant, certain, and far less expensive.

By the turn of the century or very shortly after, almost all of India's 600,000 villages will have telephone service. Once in place, the village telephone becomes as critical as water, food, shelter, and health services. Once exposed, people in rural areas want a village telephone more than they want any other community service.

Of nearly equal importance for me, the community phone becomes an instrument of social change, fundamental to the process of democratization. With telecommunications networks now spreading across the Second and Third Worlds, I believe that no amount of effort can put information back in the hands of the few, to be isolated, concentrated, and controlled.

Follow-up Now answer this question:

> Does the author appreciate technology more for its technical benefits or its social implications?

Reading for more detail

Read the selection again. Mark any places in the text that are still unclear to you.

D Helping each other understand

Write for about 20 minutes on this selection. Write about one or more of the questions below.

1. What do you have trouble understanding?
2. Do you agree with Pitroda about the importance of technology?
3. What might the Dalai Lama think of Pitroda's views?

Follow-up To a small group of students, read what you have written. Each group member will respond with (1) a question, (2) a comment, and/or (3) help with what you didn't understand.

E Discussion: Critical thinking

Discuss these questions in pairs, in small groups, or as a class.

1. Although born and raised in India, Pitroda has studied and worked in the West. Does his thinking reflect his Indian background or his U.S. experience more? Explain.
2. Is the Dalai Lama as concerned about social change as Pitroda is? Would the Dalai Lama agree with Pitroda's view that technology is a great social leveler, that it "can put unequal human beings on an equal footing"? Explain.
3. Both authors obviously care very much about people. In what ways is their caring similar? Different?
4. Does following tradition result in a more moral life than introducing technology?

PART 4

FOCUS ON WRITING SKILLS

A Using another's writing: Summarizing main ideas

Whether you agree with the Dalai Lama or not, you may want to use his ideas in the argument essay you will write in Part 5 of this chapter. A summary in your own words of his ideas in "Modern Society and the Quest for Human Happiness" would allow you to use his ideas in a concise form and in an academically honest way.

EXERCISE 1 *Summarizing the Dalai Lama selection*

Summarize the Dalai Lama selection (pages 169–171) in 125 words or less, focusing on his main ideas. Follow these steps:

1 Review the article first, and take notes of key words and ideas.

2 Begin your first draft of your summary with a general statement of his thesis.

3 Think of five major points that support that thesis. Include these in your summary.

4 Revise your first draft for accuracy and conciseness.

Follow-up Exchange summaries with a classmate. Read and compare your summaries. Did you both include the same major points?

B Meeting reader expectations: Avoiding logical fallacies

There are three good reasons to avoid logical fallacies in your writing. First, logical fallacies are wrong and, simply put, dishonest if you use them knowingly. Second, they take away from the strength of your argument. Finally, the use of logical fallacies can make your readers feel that you do not consider them to be very intelligent.

EXERCISE 2 *Recognizing logical fallacies*

Read the descriptions of the different kinds of logical fallacies in Part A. Then read each statement in Part B, and decide which kind of logical fallacy it contains. Label it with the appropriate letter. Use each letter once.

Part A: Kinds of logical fallacies

a. *False cause* Most problems are too complicated to have one simple cause. A sequence of events (one following another) does not prove that one event caused another; logical evidence does.

b. *Sweeping generalization* The writer asserts or states a general truth by implying that it is supported by authority. The implication is that there are no differences of opinion among the authorities.

c. *Circular reasoning* The assertion is not supported; it is simply repeated.

d. *Begging the question* Instead of proving that something is true, the writer simply asserts that it is true. Statements such as "It is common knowledge that . . ." are typical of this kind of fallacy.

e. *Faulty analogy* The analogy (comparison) may not be a good one because there are more differences than similarities between the two items being compared.

f. *Emotional appeal* The writer appeals to deep biases many people have for certain things (country, family) or against others (homosexuality, abortion). The fallacy excites people's emotions; it does not deal with the factual issues.

Part B: Logical fallacies

_____ 1 Those people can't be trusted because everything they do proves they're dishonest.

_____ 2 Space exploration is as important as Columbus' voyage to the new world was.

_____ 3 The increase in cancer in our community must be the result of the nuclear reactor recently built nearby.

_____ 4 Everyone knows that national health care has failed in Canada.

_____ 5 How can we elect as governor a woman who does not believe in God?

_____ 6 Scientific research has proven that global warming will destroy our planet.

EXERCISE 3 *Fixing logical fallacies*

Some of the fallacies in Part B of Exercise 2 cannot be corrected because they are based on false assumptions or premises. Others, with some thought and editing, can be changed into logical arguments. Follow the directions below to rewrite the statements to improve the logic.

1 Rewrite sentence 3 to make clear that the nuclear reactor could be one of several factors leading to the increased cancer rate.

2 Rewrite sentence 4 to make it clear that most Canadians and many U.S. experts believe Canada's system is successful even though elective medical procedures may be harder to get in Canada than in the United States.

3 Rewrite sentence 5 to present a logical reason for not electing the woman rather than making an emotional appeal.

4 Rewrite sentence 6 so that it is clear that only some (and not all) authorities support the assertion.

EXERCISE 4 *Identifying and correcting logical fallacies*

With a partner, read these statements on the topic of developing countries. Which ones contain logical fallacies? Mark statements containing fallacies with an *X*. Then discuss what makes it a fallacy and how you could correct it.

_____ 1 Developing countries must industrialize, or they will never develop.

_____ 2 Every sensible person knows that a little more pollution is the price we have to pay for material progress.

_____ 3 International aid is essential to developing nations because they cannot modernize without outside help.

_____ 4 It is obvious to any intelligent person that political problems are far more important than economic problems in today's world.

_____ 5 Politicians cannot be trusted to do the right thing because they are all corrupt.

_____ 6 Since developed countries caused the inequality among nations, they have an obligation to solve the problem.

_____ 7 Experts agree that education is the key to developing a country.

Follow-up Discuss your answers with another pair of partners or the class.

EXERCISE 5 *Student model of an argument essay*

This essay by a Mexican student is an example of an argument essay, the kind of essay you will write in Part 5 of this chapter. Read the paper the first time to answer these questions:

1 Has Mr. Orozco convinced you of his thesis?

2 Does he avoid logical fallacies in his paper?

Then read the paper a second time to answer the questions that follow it.

Francisco Orozco

What Is Quality of Life?

When people have the great experience of living in other countries, they can perceive how different the inhabitants' values and lives are from those in their own countries. In some countries, people base their quality of life on the amount of material goods they have. Most individuals in these countries base their welfare on the accumulation of money, goods, and services. To be sure, infrastructure, technology, and material progress have brought to these people a higher standard of living. In other countries, material factors play a smaller role in the quality of life. People in these countries judge that their traditions and folklore, education,

continued

and social relations are the most important qualities in their lives. Development is inevitable in every country, but as we develop, we must remember that the quality of life of individuals has two sides. When we talk about improving a country's quality of life, we should consider individuals living comfortably and fulfilling both material and spiritual needs. It is a mistake to look only at the material side and to ignore the spiritual side when considering quality of life.

On the spiritual side, quality of life means that people enjoy life the best way possible while having spare time for their families and friends. A country that stresses spiritual matters as quality of life has the advantage of creating a peaceful, secure environment for people to live in. People have enough time to share with others and learn about art, music, and traditions. They also find themselves useful to others and do the things they like without feeling the necessity to make more money than they need. A country that emphasizes nonmaterial factors may also have disadvantages such as slower progress and poor development. There is sometimes not enough money to build and create the infrastructure that inhabitants need.

In other countries, where a higher standard of living is the primary goal, it seems that everything around people ends up in monetary transactions. Personal economic growth seems to be an important issue for most people. On the positive side, a higher standard of living brings through our doors new technologies like TVs, VCRs, computers, fax machines, kitchen appliances, and so on. We also have social and medical services that make our lives more comfortable. On the other hand, a higher standard of living can bring us a number of bothersome consequences like unemployment, inflation, and a rising crime rate, all of which are evidence that a developed country is not 100 percent secure. In addition, social relations are often poor because people don't have time to talk and listen to their neighbors.

An experience of mine in southern Mexico has helped me to understand that quality of life consists of more than modern material goods. It was interesting to observe how spiritual matters were more significant than anything else in this small town. I looked at people in the streets talking to each other about their experiences and life. I saw handicrafts made by people who inherited the crafts from their ancestors. I heard musicians playing in the streets, and in the market I saw people trading what they didn't need for things they really did need. All the people had smiles on their faces and the time to talk to each other without stress or any rush. Mothers had time to attend to their children and teach them what had been passed down from generation to generation. Education was important for them too. In fact, one mother's priority each day was to send her children off to school and to supervise their homework. It was interesting to see how happily the people in this town lived despite their material poverty. Their reliance on a traditional life resulted for them in a more stable society than any governed by money and goods.

continued

When we talk about development, we talk about human progress with its positive and negative consequences. We should not forget that development does not start with goods. Rather, as Schumacher points out, it starts with people and their education, with organization, and with discipline (Schumacher, page 168). All three require time and effort to succeed. However, even more important than development is the quality of life of the people and the strong social structure it provides. A good quality of life and a strong social structure, which depend as much on the spiritual as on the material, provide social welfare, the goal of every society. At the same time they provide the foundation on which to build as the society develops and prospers.

Work Cited

Schumacher, E.F. *Small Is Beautiful: Economics As If People Mattered.* New York: Harper & Row, Publishers, Inc., 1973.

1. What is Mr. Orozco's argument, or thesis?
2. Does he present both sides of the argument? Where?
3. Does he make clear which side of the argument he prefers? If so, in which paragraph?
4. Does the introduction catch your interest and make you want to read on?
5. What point does he make in the conclusion? Does the conclusion leave you thinking about his thesis?
6. Which paragraph shows the writer's voice the most strongly?

Sentence grammar: Parallelism

PARALLEL FORMS

When ideas are presented in the same grammatical form they are said to be *parallel*. Parallelism makes writing easier to read and understand. Look at the sentences below. The sentences marked *wrong* contain items that are not grammatically parallel. These sentences are harder to read and understand because they contain grammatical forms that do not match.

WRONG   a. He would rather *swim* than *to jog* for exercise.

CORRECT   b. He would rather *swim* than *jog* for exercise.

WRONG   c. Early to bed, early to rise, makes a man *healthy, wealthy,* and *gives him wisdom*.

CORRECT   d. Early to bed, early to rise, makes a man *healthy, wealthy,* and *wise*.

WRONG   e. A lot of students attend community colleges because of the <u>low tuition, small class size, and the instructors all have professional status</u>.

CORRECT f. A lot of students attend community colleges because of the low tuition, small class size, and professional status of the instructors.

EXERCISE 6 *Making segments parallel*

In each sentence underline the segment that is not parallel. Then rewrite the sentence, revising for parallelism. Sometimes there is more than one solution; choose the solution that gives the shortest, clearest sentence.

1. India is the seventh largest country in the world in area but second in terms of how many people live there.

2. India's population is distributed unevenly, with four-fifths living in villages, and the rest live in towns and cities.

3. India's climate varies from tropical heat in the South to the North Rajasthan Desert, where they have near-Arctic cold.

4. Geographical features include the highest mountains in the world, the Himalayas, and the Ganges Plain is among the most densely populated regions of the world.

5. India's cultural heritage, including architecture, dance, literature, music, philosophy, and sculpture, is one of the richest in the world, and it is very, very ancient, too.

EXERCISE 7 *More practice in making segments parallel*

In each sentence underline the segment that is not parallel. Then rewrite the sentence, revising for parallelism. There is more than one solution for most sentences; choose the solution that gives a shorter, clearer sentence.

1. The workforce numbers 286 million people, but this figure does not include the unemployed, and secondary workers are not counted in this figure either.

2. Secondary workers, who do not receive their main support from their work activities, include people involved in household industry, and cultivation is another category of secondary workers.

3. According to a recent census, more than 67 percent of the workforce was employed in agriculture, 15 percent were factory workers, and 18 percent in services.

4. In recent decades India has experienced a "brain drain" of educated and trained Indians to other countries because of unemployment, and because underemployment was also a problem.

5. Many educated Indians prefer to seek jobs abroad or working in foreign companies located in India.

EXERCISE 8 *Editing for parallelism*

Read through this paragraph, and mark segments that are not parallel in structure. Then rewrite the paragraph, correcting the mistakes in parallelism.

   In his discussion of developing countries, Schumacher says that dual economies create political problems, and tensions arise in society, too. Every country has poor people and those that are very rich. However, in a dual economy, the difference between the two groups is so great that a cultural gap develops between the two groups. The rich, a small percentage, typically live in the capital or are inhabitants of the second largest city. The poor live in the country or are town dwellers. The problem is that most development efforts go to the big cities and help the rich. The gap between the poor and people with money increases as the rich benefit from the changes and the poor do not.

(Adapted from Small Is Beautiful: Economics as if People Mattered, *by E. F. Schumacher, Harper & Row, Publishers, Inc.)*

PART 5
FORMAL WRITING ASSIGNMENT

A Writing topics

For this writing assignment, you will write an argument essay. In this essay you will present both sides of an issue and take a position on one side or the other. Choose an essay topic from the list below, and think about your position on the issue.

1. Poorer countries should emphasize/de-emphasize technology as they move toward the future.

2. A country's quality of life is more/less important than its gross national product.

3. New technology and the traditional elements of a culture can/cannot exist together.

B Generating ideas: A debate

Follow the instructions below to hold a debate on this proposition:

Modernization is more important for a country than the preservation of its traditional life.

PREPARATION FOR THE DEBATE

To debate, you need two small groups of students. The first group will argue the *pro* position (for the proposition). The other group will argue the *con* position (against the proposition). The rest of the class will judge the debate.

The pro and con teams should meet separately to discuss their arguments, making sure to avoid logical fallacies. Each group should choose a captain. Each team member should construct a different one-to-two-minute argument to present to the class.

DEBATE

Follow these steps for the debate.

1. The captain of the pro team presents his or her argument to the class in 2 minutes or less. The con team then has two minutes to ask questions intended to show weaknesses in the argument or fallacies in the logic.

2. The captain of the con team presents his or her argument and the pro team members have two minutes to ask questions.

3. Pro and con team members continue to take turns speaking until all team members have spoken.

4 At the end, both teams have five minutes to prepare summaries of their arguments. The captain of each team will deliver the summary in two minutes or less.

DECISION

Students watching the debate can vote to decide which team presented the strongest, most logical arguments. Students should vote for the team that showed the strongest debating skills, not for the side they agree with.

Follow-up All students take 5 minutes to make lists of the best arguments for and against the proposition. These lists might be useful in writing an argument essay later.

C Expanding your point of view: Group discussion

Go over the list of arguments you wrote down after the debate. Circle the arguments that relate to your writing topic, both *for* and *against*.

Form a group with other students in your class who have chosen the same topic. Share your arguments orally. Your purpose is not to reach agreement but to share your points of view. At the end of the discussion, make any adjustments you would like to the *for* or *against* lists of arguments you have prepared for your topic.

D Initial drafts

FIRST DRAFT

Once you know your position on the issue you have chosen, formulate the thesis statement for your essay. Remember that you are writing an argument paper. As with the persuasive essay you wrote in Chapter 6, you will want to use logical evidence to support your position. However, your purpose is not merely to persuade but also to refute the opposing view. (Reread the student essay in Part 4, Section B for an example of this structure.) Therefore, the body of your essay should include your *thesis* and the *antithesis*. In the final body paragraph, you will bring the two sides together in a *synthesis* of the two, showing why your position is the more logical and better one.

You may choose to prepare an outline or write your first draft freely. Use whichever approach works best for you. Keep a balance among the body paragraphs: Avoid having one paragraph very long (your position, for example) and the next very short (the opposing side). Avoid logical fallacies.

REVISION

Have someone outside of your class read your paper to see if you have (1) expressed your position clearly, (2) explained the opposing view, and then (3) shown why your position is stronger. Ask your reader to orally summarize these parts of your paper to make sure they are clear.

You may choose to rewrite portions of the essay depending on your friend's comments. Revise your first draft following the *Essay Assessment Guidelines* at the end of this chapter; label this draft "Draft 2."

Ⓔ Review, revision, and assessment

 PEER FEEDBACK

Read a classmate's paper, and give feedback using the *Essay Assessment Checklist* on page 189. Write your comments on the checklist, but make no marks on your classmate's paper. Give the checklist and the paper back to the writer. Answer any questions your classmate has about your feedback.

FURTHER REVISION

What did you learn from the feedback you received? Is your essay successful—is it convincing, interesting, clearly organized, and complete? If not, how can you make it more successful?

Revise your paper using the feedback you got in class. Give your teacher all drafts (with the last draft marked "Final draft") and the *Essay Assessment Checklist* completed by your classmate.

Writer's name: _____

Reader's name: _____

Essay Assessment Checklist   Chapter 7

These are the criteria for a well-written argument essay. Use them to examine your writing, or a classmate's, and check *Yes* or *No* for each item. You may wish to add comments or suggestions.

Content and ideas

	Yes	No	Reader's comments
1 The writer has thought carefully about the topic and understands both sides of the argument.	☐	☐	
2 The writer presents both sides of the argument adequately and then convinces us why his or her position is stronger.	☐	☐	
3 The writer's voice is clear because he or she writes in a sincere way and keeps the audience in mind.	☐	☐	
4 The reader wants to continue reading to the end. It's interesting.	☐	☐	

Organization and form

	Yes	No	
5 The writer presents the thesis, the antithesis, and a synthesis of the two positions in order and in separate paragraphs.	☐	☐	
6 The essay moves logically in a straight line. The reader can understand the thesis and support fully after one reading.	☐	☐	

Language

	Yes	No	
7 The paper is easy to understand. These elements are used well:			
• sentence structure	☐	☐	
• grammar	☐	☐	
• vocabulary	☐	☐	
• mechanics (spelling, capitalization, punctuation)	☐	☐	
• consistency in tense, person, number, and tone	☐	☐	
• parallelism	☐	☐	

APPENDIX A

MORE ON GRAMMAR AND PUNCTUATION

1 SENTENCE STRUCTURE

A General sentence structure

Analyze the example sentences in the chart below. They all express the same meaning, but the sentence structure and punctuation vary. Coordinating conjunctions, subordinating conjunctions, transition words, and prepositions all function differently.

Example sentences	Sentence structure
1 I was tired, *but* I went on studying.	**Compound:** two independent clauses joined by a coordinating conjunction (*but*).
2 *Although* I was tired, I went on studying. —or— I went on studying *although* I was tired.	**Complex:** a dependent clause with a subordinating conjunction (*although*), joined to an independent clause.
3 I was tired; *however*, I went on studying.	**Compound:** two independent clauses joined by a transition word (*however*).
4 *In spite of being tired*, I went on studying. —or— I went on studying *in spite of being tired*.	**Simple:** one independent clause with a prepositional phrase (*in spite of being tired*).

EXERCISE 1 *Identifying sentence structure*

Read the sentences in each group below. Circle the letter of every correct sentence in the group. Sentences in the same group should express the same meaning.

1. a. I'll go with you although I'm busy tonight.
   b. Even though I'm busy tonight, I'll go with you.
   c. I'll go with you tonight in spite of I am busy.
   d. I'm quite busy; however, I'll go with you tonight.
   e. Although I'm busy, but I'll go with you tonight.
   f. In spite of being busy, I'll go with you tonight.

2. a. Due to the weather, I'm staying home tonight.
   b. Because it's very windy, I'm staying home tonight.
   c. Because of it's windy, I'm staying home tonight.

d. It's very windy outside; therefore, I'm staying home tonight.

   e. It's very windy outside, so I'm staying home tonight.

3 a. In spite of the difficulty of the book, Allie finished it.

   b. Even though it was a difficult book, Allie finished it.

   c. Allie finished reading the book despite the difficulty.

   d. It was a difficult book, however; Allie finished it.

4 a. George was an architect. Before that, he was a draftsman.

   b. George was an architect before he was a draftsman.

   c. George was an architect; formerly, he was a draftsman.

   d. First, George was a draftsman; then he was an architect.

   e. Before becoming an architect, George was a draftsman.

Note: In less formal usage, to avoid very long sentences, writers sometimes use coordinating conjunctions (*and, or, but, yet, for, nor*) to begin a second sentence.

   a. It was a difficult book. *But* Ben finished it.

Transition words can be used in the same way, in formal or informal usage:

   b. It was a difficult book. *However*, Ben finished it.

B Transition words

Study how transition words work in the example sentences in the chart. Transition words are in *italics*. Sometimes transition words are conjunctions that join independent clauses into one compound sentence. Sometimes they show the relationship between two separate sentences. Note the punctuation in each example.

Example sentences	*Sentence structure*
1 Finish your dinner; *afterwards*, I'll take you to the movies.	**Compound:** two independent clauses joined by a transition word (*afterwards*).
2 a. Finish your dinner. *Afterwards*, I'll take you to the movies. b. Finish your dinner. *Then* I'll take you to the movies. c. Finish your dinner. I'll take you to the movies *afterwards*.	**Simple:** two sentences whose meanings are connected with a transition word (*afterwards, then*).
3 Finish your dinner, and *afterwards*, I'll take you to the movies.	**Compound:** two independent clauses joined by a coordinating conjunction (*and*) with a transition word (*afterwards*).
4 We ate dinner, went to the movies, and *then* came home.	**Simple:** a sentence with three verbs (*ate, went, came*) joined by *and* with a transition word (*then*).

The sentence below expresses the same idea as example sentence *2c* in the chart, using the subordinating conjunction *after* instead of the transition word *afterwards*. Compare the structures of the two sentences.

<u>After</u> you finish your dinner, I'll take you to the movies.

Note: (1) Transition words can often move to any position in their clause. They are usually followed by a comma. However, short transition words like *then* and *now* are usually not followed by commas. (2) Transition words cannot join two independent clauses with only a comma. They join two clauses into a sentence (or connect ideas in two sentences) in the ways shown in the example sentences on page 192.

EXERCISE 2 *Identifying correct structure and punctuation*

Read the sentences in each group. Circle the letter of every sentence in the group that has good sentence structure and punctuation. Sentences in the same group should express the same meaning. Transition words are in italics.

1. a. I read for a while. After I listened to music.
   b. I read for a while. *Afterwards,* I listened to music.
   c. I read for a while, *after that,* I listened to music.
   d. I read for a while, and *then* I listened to music.

2. a. She's a wonderful student, but she doesn't always turn in work on time.
   b. She's a wonderful student, *however,* she doesn't always turn in work on time.
   c. She's a wonderful student; she doesn't always turn in work on time, *however.*
   d. She's a wonderful student. She doesn't, *however,* always turn in work on time.

3. a. We went out to eat, *then* we had coffee, *finally* we went home.
   b. We went out to eat. *Then* we had coffee, and *finally* we went home.
   c. We went out to eat, and *then* we had coffee. *Finally,* we went home.
   d. We went out to eat, *then* we had coffee, and *finally* we went home.
   e. After we had dinner, we had coffee and *then* went home.

2 RELATIVE CLAUSES

Relative clauses are dependent clauses that modify the nouns they follow. The relative clause comes right after the noun. In the example below, relative clauses are in *italics*, the nouns they modify are underlined.

a. The <u>book</u> *that I needed* was not available in the college bookstore.
b. The <u>woman</u> *who runs the bookstore* said the book would be available two weeks from now.
c. Unfortunately, the <u>assignments</u> *our teacher has given us* require reading the book right away.

d. The <u>town</u> *where I was born* has not changed much over the years.

e. The <u>woman</u> *to whom he's married* has a successful career as a doctor.

f. I don't know <u>anyone</u> *whose life is free of problems*.

g. <u>Professor Chen</u>, *whom you all know well,* has published a new book.

GUIDELINES FOR RELATIVE CLAUSES

Guideline 1

The relative pronouns *who* and *that* are used for people; *which* and *that* are used for things. *Whose* is the possessive relative pronoun; it takes the place of possessive adjectives in a relative clause (see example *d*). In formal writing, *whom* is often used in place of *who* when it is the object of a verb or the object of a preposition in a relative clause (see examples *e* and *f*).

a. The person *who lost his keys* is waiting outside.

b. The book *that you are looking at* is very expensive.

c. Montreal is a city *which is known for its good food.*

d. I can't find the student *whose parents just arrived from Indonesia.* (not *who his parents . . .*)

e. The man *to whom you explained the contract* has some questions about it.

f. Mahatma Gandhi, *whom the world respected for his peaceful ways,* still inspires people today.

Guideline 2

A relative clause is either restrictive or nonrestrictive. A restrictive clause restricts, or limits, the meaning of the noun it modifies; it tells you *which one* (or ones) is being talked about. Restrictive clauses are essential to the meaning of the main clause and are not set off with commas. If you take away the restrictive clause, the sentence loses an essential part of its meaning.

RESTRICTIVE   Most foreign students *who don't study hard* don't pass the TOEFL.

It is a fact that most foreign students do pass the TOEFL. Without the relative clause, the sentence is not factually correct, so the clause is restrictive, or essential. The clause is not set apart by commas.

Nonrestrictive clauses are not essential to the meaning of the main clause, so they are set off with commas. Nonrestrictive clauses do not use *that* as a relative pronoun and never omit the relative pronoun. To test if a clause is restrictive, ask yourself, "Does the sentence still make sense without the clause?" If not, then the clause is necessary—and restrictive. If yes, then the clause is extra information—and nonrestrictive.

NONRESTRICTIVE   Foreign students, *who must have student visas to study at U.S. universities,* add diversity and a new perspective to U.S. campuses.

The relative clause is nonrestrictive because it is extra, nonessential information; the sentence makes perfect sense without the clause.

Guideline 3
The relative pronoun is often omitted in restrictive clauses where the relative pronoun is an object of a preposition or verb.

- a. Most of the people *I went to school with* are quite successful.
  (The omitted relative pronoun *whom* is the object of the preposition *with*.)
- b. I can't find the tickets *we bought*.
  (The omitted relative pronoun *that* is the direct object of the verb *bought*.)

Guideline 4
Subjects and objects are not repeated in a relative clause even when the relative pronoun is omitted. The verb in a relative clause agrees with its logical subject.

WRONG	a. Have you found the keys *you lost them*?
CORRECT	b. Have you found the keys *you lost*?
WRONG	c. It's odd that people *who they seem smart* can be so forgetful.
CORRECT	d. It's odd that people *who seem smart* can be so forgetful.
WRONG	e. Is there anything *which are more important than health*?
CORRECT	f. Is there anything *which is more important than health*?

(The singular pronoun *anything* is the logical subject of the relative clause.)

Guideline 5
Prepositions (*to, of, about,* and so on) and quantity expressions (*many, half, some,* and so on) are sometimes needed to complete or limit the meaning of a relative clause:

- a. The person *you're speaking <u>to</u>* isn't the one *we're supposed to see*.
- b. Politics is not a subject <u>*about*</u> *which he knows very much*.
- c. When Mrs. Grimes died, she left a lot of money, <u>*half*</u> *of which she gave to charity*.

Note: Example *a*, with the preposition *to* in final position in the clause, is acceptable in both spoken and written usage. Example *b*, with the preposition in initial position, is quite formal.

Guideline 6
Where as a relative pronoun introduces the meaning of *there* into a relative clause. Compare these two sentences:

- a. They visited the city *where* they were married. (They were married *there*.)
- b. They visited the city *that* had been hit by an earthquake. (*It* had been hit.)

EXERCISE 3 *Recognizing good relative clauses*

Underline the relative clause in each sentence. Put a check (✔) in the blank if the sentence is grammatically correct and has correct punctuation. Put an ✗ in the blank if it is incorrect. Correct the incorrect relative clauses.

_____ 1 The city water department needs a secretary who can do word processing.

_____ 2 A penalty will be added to bills which is paid late.

_____ 3 I bought some notebooks on sale which they are not of very good quality.

_____ 4 When is that library book we used for our report due?

_____ 5 Professor Chavez, who you know as the author of our economics text, will deliver a guest lecture next Friday.

_____ 6 He is a good speaker who his accomplishments are known to all.

_____ 7 Can you recommend a restaurant who serves fish?

_____ 8 Can you recommend a restaurant where fish is served?

_____ 9 Firefighters whose work can be very dangerous are often paid less than police officers or aren't paid at all.

_____ 10 I'm afraid that the cassette I am listening to it is defective. Can I get another copy?

_____ 11 It is sometimes difficult to convince students who their only goal is to pass the TOEFL that ability is more important than test results.

_____ 12 Is that the company you wrote your letter of complaint to?

_____ 13 I removed an egg from a carton that was damaged.

Follow-up Write two sentences illustrating each of the six guidelines. Write about your English studies.

EXERCISE 4 *Adding relative clauses to sentences*

Read each sentence. Then decide which of the two clauses in parentheses is a well-formed relative clause that correctly modifies a noun in the sentence. Rewrite the sentence, inserting this clause. (Commas indicate a nonrestrictive relative clause.)

1 Professor Norris is an excellent administrator.
   a. (, who used to direct the English language program,)
   b. (that is the author of our textbook)

2 Computers are becoming more widespread worldwide.
   a. (, which have come down in price,)
   b. (they are beneficial in education)

3 The police haven't been able to locate the witness.
   a. (her testimony is important to the case)
   b. (, whose testimony is important to the case)

4 I would like a car.
   a. (that it can hold five or six passengers)
   b. (that doesn't require a lot of maintenance)

5 The book bag isn't big enough for all the books I need this semester.
   a. (I bought)
   b. (that are quite useful)

6 People shouldn't throw stones.
   a. (who live in glass houses)
   b. (, who live in glass houses,)

7 Students usually find that their writing improves.
   a. (they like to read)
   b. (who read a lot)

8 Punctuation is not terribly difficult to learn to use correctly.
   a. (, which often frustrates writing students,)
   b. (that students don't like)

9 I gave him the letter.
   a. (he asked for)
   b. (he asked for it)

10 My sister-in-law is coming to visit soon.
    a. (, who I introduced you to once,)
    b. (to which I introduced you once)

11 We bought two kilograms of rice.
    a. (, some of it wasn't very good)
    b. (, most of which we'll prepare for the party)

12 We've invited a lot of people to the party.
    a. (most of them you've met)
    b. (, most of whom you know,)

13 They want to go someplace.
    a. (, they can be alone there)
    b. (where they can be alone)

14 Pam gave me a lot of advice.

   a. (which weren't very good)

   b. (, most of which wasn't useful)

3 WORD ORDER

English word order is rigid compared to word order in many other languages. The following section contains a review of the correct placement of adverbials, modifiers, the words *also* and *too,* and direct and indirect objects.

A Adverbials

GUIDELINES FOR ADVERBIALS

Guideline 1
A verb and its direct object are almost never separated.

WRONG   a. I like very much your new hat.
        (The adverbial *very much* cannot come between the verb and its direct object.)

CORRECT b. I like your new hat very much.

Guideline 2
Adverbs of frequency (*always, often, seldom, never,* and so on) come after *be* or the first auxiliary verb if there is one. However, these adverbs come before other verbs, even in the negative.

   a. My sister <u>is</u> *never* on time for appointments.

   b. We <u>have</u> *often* had lunch there on weekends.

   c. <u>Aren't</u> they *usually* late with their rent check?

   d. Sally *seldom* <u>writes</u> to me anymore.

   e. I <u>didn't</u> *always* hand in my homework on time.

Guideline 3
Other adverbials typically come at the end of the sentence in this order:
(1) manner (how), (2) place, and (3) time.

   Jim does his homework   alone   at home   after class.
                          manner **place**   **time**

Exceptions
The frequency adverbs *sometimes* and *usually* and adverbials of time can come at the beginning of a sentence.

a. *Sometimes* I like to sleep late on weekends.

b. *This past winter*, we had higher than normal heating bills.

The negative frequency adverbs *never, rarely,* and *seldom* can also come at the beginning of a sentence, but are then followed by inverted word order:

c. *Never* have I seen such a huge watermelon before!
          V. S.

d. *Seldom* does he help his wife with the housework.
          V. S.

e. *Rarely* have I felt so embarrassed.
        V. S.

The word order given in Guideline 2 is more common, however, and more informal.

EXERCISE 5 *Using adverbials*

Divide the following adverbs and adverbial phrases into three groups: *manner, place,* and *time.* Then write five sentences, each of which contains two of these adverbials. Use Guidelines 1–3 to help you determine the correct placement of these words and phrases.

since Monday	in a hurry
punctually	at home
without looking	on my birthday
late	recently
to the store	here
carelessly	on campus
early	meaningfully

EXERCISE 6 *Correct word order*

Form sentences by putting the words in the correct order. Use every word. Use question word order for items followed by a question mark.

1. his / doesn't / brush / he / after meals / always / teeth / .
2. time / at home / have / seldom / on weekdays / lunch / I / to cook / .
3. rarely / in my country / snows / in the winter / it / .
4. his / in a restaurant / at night / they / birthday / celebrate / usually / with a big party / .
5. on the weekend / ever / you / do / with friends / to the movies / go / ?
6. his strange behavior / to understand / I / the reason / never / been able / have / for / .
7. likely / George / is / at home / again / to leave / his homework / ?
8. in a quiet place / don't / I / without interruptions / usually / trouble / doing my homework / have / .
9. too many / in line / aren't / at the post office / right now / people / there / .

10 has / she / to go out / never / on the weekend / with them / wanted / .

11 time / to read / have / seldom / stories / do / a second time / I / .

12 experienced / I / never / rude behavior / such / had / .

B Modifiers

A modifier is a word or phrase that adds to the meaning of other words. Modifiers can change the meaning of a sentence by changing the meaning of one word in the sentence. Consider these examples with the adverbs *only, almost,* and *even*:

   a. *Only* Susan said she liked spaghetti. (The others said they didn't like spaghetti.)
   b. Susan *only said* she like spaghetti. (She doesn't like it; she just said so to spare her mother-in-law's feelings.)
   c. Susan said she liked *only* spaghetti. (She doesn't care to eat anything else.)
   d. I *almost spent* $100 on new shoes. (I was close to buying the shoes for $100, but I didn't.)
   e. I spent *almost $100* on new shoes. (The shoes I bought cost close to $100.)
   f. *Even* I finished the homework. (I don't usually finish it, but this time I did, just like the other students.)
   g. I *even finished* the homework. (I accomplished a lot tonight; finishing my homework was one of my many accomplishments.)

Relative clauses and prepositional phrases also function as modifiers. And like the adverbs just discussed, their placement in the sentence affects the meaning of the sentence:

   h. I pushed an emergency button *that didn't work* in the elevator. (The button didn't work.)
   i. I pushed an emergency button in the *elevator that didn't work*. (The elevator didn't work.)
   j. The teacher explained the error to the *student with a smile on his face*. (The student was smiling.)
   k. *With a smile on his face, the teacher* explained the error to the student. (The teacher was smiling.)

EXERCISE 7 *Adding modifiers to sentences*

Read the sentences and add the modifiers in parentheses.

1 (almost) I dropped my book on the floor.

2 (that are dependent) Children need their parents.

3 (nearly) It took most of the students three hours to write their compositions.

4 (only) Some of them spent 30 minutes doing it.

5 (that was so difficult) The students did not appreciate another assignment from their teacher.

6 (even) This task is so simple that a three-year-old can do it.

7 (without looking at them) The teacher asked a question of the students, who answered quickly.

8 (that smelled wonderful) The cosmetic salesperson sprayed perfume samples on the customer.

9 (hardly) Mary's unhealthy because she eats anything.

10 (only) A mother knows what her children are really like.

C Also and too

Also usually goes before a single-word main verb, but after *be* and after the first auxiliary. *Too* goes at the end of the clause and is preceded by a comma.

a. They've registered for their required classes. They *also* want to register for a gym class.

b. Not only is he my cousin, he is *also* my friend.

c. Carl's grandparents will *also* come to visit him.

d. You will have to do homework and be ready for an exam, *too*.

EXERCISE 8 *Adding* also *and* too

Read the two sentences in each item. Insert the word in parentheses into the second sentence.

1 (too) Tony took his parents sightseeing last weekend. He took them to his favorite restaurant.

2 (also) His parents liked the places they visited. They liked the food at the restaurant.

3 (also) His parents usually visit Tony in May. This year they are coming in September.

4 (too) The Johnsons stay at a hotel when they visit Tony because he has a small apartment. He has a roommate.

5 (too) Tony is looking forward to their next visit. His aunt and uncle are going to visit.

6 (also) His parents usually drive when they visit. His aunt and uncle will drive, but in their own car.

7 (also) Tony likes his uncle a lot. He likes his aunt, but not as much.

D Direct and indirect objects

When both direct and indirect objects accompany a verb, there are two possible patterns for most verbs:

Pattern 1
This pattern consists of the verb (V.) followed by the direct object (D.O.), the preposition *to* or *for*, and the indirect object (I.O.).

    a. I wrote a letter to my best friend last night.
       V.   D.O.   I.O.

    b. My father bought a car for me.
         V. D.O. I.O.

Use *to* with indirect objects after verbs like *give, lend, bring, send, write,* and *tell*. Use *for* with indirect objects after verbs like *buy, get,* and *make*.

Pattern 2
This pattern consists of the verb followed by the indirect object followed by the direct object.

    a. I wrote my best friend a letter last night.
       V.   I.O.   D.O.

    b. My father bought me a car.
         V. I.O. D.O.

Exceptions
When the direct object is a pronoun, only Pattern 1 is possible.

    a. I sent it to my cousin last month.
      V. D.O.   I.O.

    b. He got it for me at a discount.
      V. D.O. I.O.

Some verbs, like *say, explain,* and *recommend,* take only Pattern 1.

    c. He didn't say "Good morning" to me.
        V.   D.O.   I.O.

    d. Jeff explained his problem to her.
        V.   D.O.   I.O.

    e. Can you recommend a good restaurant to us?
       V.   D.O.   I.O.

EXERCISE 9 *Adding indirect objects to sentences*
Insert the indirect object in parentheses into each sentence.

1 (me) My parents didn't give what I wanted for my birthday.

2 (for me) I had asked for a particular motorcycle, but they didn't buy it.

3 (them) I was disappointed because I had told which model I wanted.

4 (me) Fortunately, several friends remembered to send cards.

5 (for me) My mother also made a cake, so I was somewhat consoled about the motorcycle.

6 (me) My parents also bought a very nice sweater.

7 (to him) A friend has really admired the sweater, but I don't think I'll ever lend it.

8 (him) I was telling the truth when I said he could borrow anything else I had.

9 (to him) After I explained the situation, he was completely understanding.

10 (for myself) I'm working part-time so that I can buy the motorcycle.

11 (to me) I really don't expect my parents to give it.

12 (to them) I'll never say anything about the motorcycle again.

EXERCISE 10 *Completing sentences with direct and indirect objects*

In each item complete the second sentence by adding both an indirect and a direct object and any other phrases or clauses necessary to complete the logic of the sentence. Use pronouns for the objects, and the prepositions *to* and *for* as needed.

1 Mary gave John some flowers. She gave _____ reluctantly because _____.

2 I'm going to send my brother a birthday card. I'll send _____ even though _____.

3 I don't understand this equation. Could you explain _____ so that _____?

4 She told me a funny story. She had to tell _____ in a soft voice because _____.

5 I hope you take better care of my notes this time. If you don't, I won't lend_____.

6 That is a very pretty sweater. Who made _____?

7 I'm going to get my parents a TV for their anniversary. I'll try to buy _____ early so that _____.

8 My books are in your car. Could you bring _____ before you _____?

9 I don't especially like that restaurant. I really can't recommend _____.

4 ADJECTIVES AND ADVERBS

Adjectives modify nouns and pronouns. They may occur just before the nouns they modify, or they may be connected to nouns and pronouns through linking verbs.

   a. The *big, healthy, blue-eyed* boxer got a *black* eye in her *last* match.
      (The adjectives occur just before the nouns.)

   b. She felt *embarrassed* and at the same time *ashamed* because she lost the fight.
      (The adjectives are connected to the pronoun *she* through the linking verb *felt*.)

Adverbs modify verbs, adjectives, or other adverbs. They usually follow the verbs they modify and precede the adjectives or adverbs they modify. Adverbs often end in *-ly*. The words being modified are underlined.

   c. Susan <u>plays</u> soccer *more skillfully* than most of her teammates.

   d. Which do you <u>like</u> *better*, coffee or tea?

   e. I'm *extremely* <u>disappointed</u> in you.

   f. He <u>did</u> his homework *very carefully*.

Ⓐ Adjectives and adverbs with the same form

Although most adverbs differ in form from their related adjectives, some share the same form.

a.	ADJECTIVE	*Fast* cars use a lot of gas.
b.	ADVERB	Jeff eats very *fast*.
c.	ADJECTIVE	I don't feel *well* today. (*Well* is an adjective when it refers to health.)
d.	ADVERB	He usually does *well* on exams.
e.	ADJECTIVE	I have an *early* appointment with the doctor.
f.	ADVERB	I'll get up a little *early* to get there on time.
g.	ADJECTIVE	This will be a *hard* case for the lawyers to win.
h.	ADVERB	They will have to work very *hard* to convince the jury.

Note: The adverb *hardly* is different from *hard* and usually precedes the main verb.

   a. I can *hardly* stay awake in that class.
      (*hardly* = barely, almost not)

   b. He knows he will succeed if he works *hard*.
      (*hard* = with great energy)

Appendix A

EXERCISE 11 *Using adjectives and adverbs*

Read each sentence and circle the correct choice for each pair of words in parentheses.

1. If you try (hard/hardly), you will (sure/surely) succeed.
2. The quiz was so (easy/easily) that I finished very (quick/quickly).
3. I'm not very (good/well) at tennis, but I swim quite (good/well).
4. You look very (handsome/handsomely) today.
5. Let's finish this assignment (quick/fast) so that we can go out.
6. He says he's got a cold, but he seems (well/finely) to me.
7. I can't treat you to lunch because I (hard/hardly) have enough money for myself.
8. The boss got (real/really) angry with the employees.
9. I will (glad/gladly) lend him my car.
10. The new boss expects the employees to work more (efficient/efficiently) than they used to.
11. She isn't as (friendly/nicely) as her brother.
12. It's better to be (safe/safely) than sorry.

B Comparative forms

Comparatives are used to compare two people or things. Adjectives and adverbs usually have different comparative forms.

Adjective	Adverb	Comparative Adjective	Comparative Adverb
slow	slowly	slower	more slowly
safe	safely	safer	more safely
nice	nicely	nicer	more nicely
easy	easily	easier	more easily
busy	busily	busier	more busily
noisy	noisily	noisier	more noisily

Exceptions:

Adjective/Adverb	Comparative Adjective/Comparative Adverb
hard	harder
early	earlier
late	later
fast	faster

EXERCISE 12 *Using comparative forms*

Read each sentence and circle the correct form in parentheses.

1. You can do this (easier/more easily) if you concentrate.
2. The (busier/more busily) he is, the more nervous he gets.
3. They moved to a (safer/more safely) neighborhood.
4. The class tends to get (noisier/more noisily) when the teacher leaves the room.
5. He's trying to live (healthier/more healthily) by eating better.
6. I'm afraid I have to ask you to work a little (quicker/more quickly).
7. Try to treat him a little (nicer/more nicely), and I'm sure he'll cooperate.
8. He is much (slower/more slowly) in reading than in math.
9. The composition was (easier/more easily) to do than I had expected.
10. They asked me to drive (slower/more slowly).

5 PUNCTUATION

A Commas

GUIDELINES FOR PUNCTUATION

Guideline 1
Use a comma after an introductory clause or phrase.

INTRODUCTORY PHRASE	a. *To be honest,* I don't know where he comes from.
INTRODUCTORY DEPENDENT CLAUSE	b. *Because it rained last night,* it's cooler today.

Guideline 2
Use commas to set off nonessential clauses and phrases.

NONESSENTIAL	a. Jeffrey, *who didn't take the final exam,* failed his biology course. (The independent clause *Jeffrey failed his biology course* makes sense without the relative clause. Commas are used to signal that the relative clause is nonrestrictive, or nonessential.)

  b. The final exam, *I assume,* will be comprehensive.
   (*I assume* interrupts the main clause but is extra information and therefore nonessential. Other similar expressions are: *of course, it seems, I think, to be sure,* and *according to the author.*)

  c. My wife, *Zelda,* earns more money than anyone else in her department.

ESSENTIAL   a. All students *who don't take the final exam* will fail the course.
   (The independent clause *All students will fail the course* does not make sense without the relative clause; the relative clause is essential and needs no commas.)

  b. My brother *Ronald* cooks better than I do.
   (The absence of commas here tells the reader that *Ronald* is essential information; therefore, the writer must have more than one brother.)

EXERCISE 13 *Using commas for introductory and nonessential elements*

Read the sentences. Add commas as needed to set off introductory phrases and clauses and nonessential elements.

1 On their vacation the Slovins are going to go to India which they've both been interested in visiting ever since an Indian family moved in next door.

2 Because of busy work schedules they won't be able to spend more than two weeks there.

3 They'll visit the Taj Mahal I'm sure as well as two or three major cities.

4 Since the Slovins live in a warm climate they already have suitable clothes for their trip.

5 They'll want to buy presents which are typical of the places that they visit.

6 In my opinion they'll have a wonderful time because both are good travelers and interested in other cultures.

 Follow-up Write two sentences illustrating Guideline 1 and two sentences illustrating Guideline 2. Write about plans for a visit to another country.

Guideline 3

Use a comma to separate two independent clauses joined by a coordinating conjunction (*and, or, but, so,* and so on).

TWO CLAUSES   a. I have a lot of homework, but I'll be able to finish it.

ONE CLAUSE, TWO VERBS   b. I'll write my report tonight and revise it tomorrow.

Guideline 4
Use commas to separate a series (three or more) of similar items.

SERIES OF SUBJECTS   a. Frank, his brother, and I are going to Mexico together.

                         b. Swimming, walking, and jogging are all good forms of exercise.

SERIES OF VERBS   c. We hope to swim, sunbathe, relax, and eat good seafood.

Note: Some writers omit the comma before *and* in a series. If you omit the final comma before *and,* do so consistently in your writing.

EXERCISE 14 *Using commas to separate independent clauses and items in a series*

Read the sentences. Add commas to separate independent clauses and items in a series.

1. Jack his brother and I are going hiking and fishing this weekend.
2. We had wanted to go to the beach but we couldn't get hotel accommodations.
3. We decided to go to the mountains instead and enjoy the cooler weather.
4. We'll probably hike for a few days and then we'll relax by fishing at the local lake.
5. We'll take food sleeping bags a few changes of clothes but little else.
6. Would you like to come along or are you busy this weekend?

Follow-up Write two sentences illustrating Guideline 3 and two illustrating Guideline 4. Write about a recent vacation.

Guideline 5
Use commas to set off items in an address or date.

    a. I was born in Chicago, Illinois, U.S.A. on February 5, 1978.

    b. Chadwick's of Boston is at 2 Chadwick Place, Brockton, Massachusetts 02303.

Note: No commas are used after the country name or between the state and the zip code.

EXERCISE 15 *Using commas in addresses and dates*

Write sentences to answer the following questions, and separate items with commas.

1. Where and when were you born?
2. Where and when were your parents or other relatives married?
3. Where and when did you send your last letter? Whom did you send it to?

B Periods, semicolons, and colons

Guideline 1
End a complete sentence with a period.

   a. He cried.

   b. She tried to comfort him.

   c. They made up.

Guideline 2
Use a semicolon to separate independent clauses that are closely related and not joined with a conjunction. This rule applies even if the second clause contains a transition word.

   a. He cried; she tried to comfort him; they made up.

   b. He cried, she tried to comfort him, and they made up.
   (No semicolon is needed because the series is joined with *and*.)

   c. He cried; therefore, she tried to comfort him.

   d. He cried, and she, therefore, tried to comfort him.
   (No semicolon is needed because the two clauses are joined with *and*.)

Guideline 3
Use a colon after a complete sentence to announce a list, a long quotation, or an explanation of the sentence.

LIST	a. You'll probably need to bring these items on the hike: a tent, a sleeping bag, and food and water for three days.
LONG QUOTATION	b. In *America as a Civilization,* Max Lerner says: "What holds America together? A democracy, De Tocqueville wrote, cannot function without a religion and a philosophy. Which is to say that while every civilization needs some principle to hold it together, a democracy has a special problem of cohesion."
EXPLANATION	c. There is something I have never understood about Jeffrey: his inability to arrive anywhere on time.

EXERCISE 16 *Using periods, semicolons, and colons*

Read these sentences. Add periods, semicolons, and colons where needed. Add capital letters if necessary.

1 Students who wish to improve their writing can do so in three ways reading more, studying English rhetoric and sentence structure, and heeding their writing teacher's comments.

2 Punctuation is not very interesting to study correct punctuation does, however, make writing easier to read.

3 The semicolon and the colon look similar and, therefore, are sometimes used incorrectly by students.

4 The period and the semicolon are almost identical in function each signals that an independent clause lies before and after it.

5 There is an important difference between the period and the semicolon the semicolon is used within one longer sentence, while the period breaks up two independent clauses into separate sentences.

6 Students should be careful to use the right transition word it is better to omit a transition word than to use it incorrectly.

7 By far the most mistakes are made with commas they are often used unnecessarily.

8 An understanding of the basic rules of punctuation and a little practice are sufficient for most students to master punctuation, however.

C Apostrophes

The apostrophe has two functions in English: It is used to replace missing letters in contractions and to indicate possession. What letter(s) does the apostrophe replace in the contractions in these examples?

a. they're
b. didn't
c. it's
d. I've

e. We'd better go.
f. She'd rather stay.
g. There's going to be a party.
h. There's been an accident.

To indicate possession with an apostrophe, follow these rules:

1 Add 's to singular nouns, indefinite nouns, and plural nouns with irregular plurals.

a. John's car
b. my father's car
c. somebody else's sweater

d. everyone's friend
e. the men's room
f. children's books

2 Add only an apostrophe to plural nouns ending in *s*.

g. the boys' room
h. the Smiths' summer house
i. ten dollars' worth of stamps

3 Add an apostrophe only or *'s* to singular nouns ending in *s*.

   j. the waitress' tips *or* the waitress's tips

   k. James' car *or* James's car

Do not use apostrophes with possessive pronouns. The possessive pronouns *its* and *whose* are easy to confuse with their homonyms *it's* (contraction for *it is*) and *who's* (contraction for *who is*).

POSSESSIVE PRONOUNS	a. Jane's composition was longer than *ours*.
	b. The others' papers got better grades than *hers* did.
CONTRACTION	c. *It's* a pretty day.
POSSESSIVE PRONOUN	d. The cloud cast *its* shadow on the lake.
CONTRACTION	e. *Who's* coming to dinner?
POSSESSIVE PRONOUN	f. He is the teacher *whose* lectures have been videotaped for TV.

EXERCISE 17 *Comparing expressions*

Working with a partner or as a class, look at each pair of correctly punctuated expressions. Explain the differences in form and meaning.

1 Joan and Mike's car / Joan's and Mike's cars

2 the boy's toys / the boys' toys

3 the waitress's uniforms / the waitresses' uniforms

4 the lady's room / the ladies' room

5 the wings of the airplane / the bird's wings

6 my brother-in-law's work / my brother-in-law's working

EXERCISE 18 *Adding apostrophes*

Read the sentences and add apostrophes where necessary.

1 Peg and Sues Diner doesnt open until eight oclock in the morning.

2 The students assignments in Professor Browns section are longer than ours.

3 My roommates class schedules are easier than mine.

4 This years winter lettuce crop was ruined by heavy rains.

5 Whose dress is Helen going to wear, yours or hers?

6 Whos going to meet Phyllis flight tomorrow night—her husband or her sons?

7 Flight attendants working hours are just as long as pilots.

D Quotation marks and indirect speech

Direct speech is someone's exact words and requires quotation marks.

DIRECT
    a. "But I hate spinach," he protested.

    b. The counselor asked, "Whom do you take after more—your mother or your father?"

Indirect speech is the writer's report of what someone said and does not have quotation marks. *That* is often used to introduce indirect statements. Questions in indirect speech occur as dependent clauses with subject-verb word order. They are reported without question marks, but the main clause can be a question that requires a question mark.

INDIRECT
    a. He protested that he hated spinach.

    b. The counselor asked whom I took after more—my mother or my father.

Guideline 1
Periods and commas go inside quotation marks.

    "Your grades will be sent to your home address," the letter said.

Guideline 2
Question marks go inside quotation marks when they apply to the quotation. They go outside quotation marks when they apply to the whole sentence.

    a. "Where do you live?" he wanted to know.

    b. Who said, "Birds of a feather flock together"?

Guideline 3
A quotation begins with a capital letter if it is a complete sentence. It also begins with a capital letter if it comes at the beginning of the sentence that it is a part of.

    "I don't care about grades," Peter said, "but I need the credits to graduate."

Guideline 4
Words such as *said, protested,* and *proclaimed,* which report a quotation, are not inside quotation marks. If these words come before the quote, they are followed by a comma.

    a. The coach proclaimed, "We have the best soccer team in the league!"

    b. "We have the best soccer team in the league!" the coach proclaimed.

EXERCISE 19 *Adding quotation marks*

Read the sentences and add quotation marks and capital letters where needed. Add necessary punctuation to all sentences.

1 He asked me where I had been living

2 I told him I have the same apartment that I had when I met you

3 Are you eating well my mother always asks when she calls and do you have nice friends

4 I assure her that I can take care of myself and that she shouldn't worry

5 The police wanted to know what we had seen during the accident

6 We said we weren't really paying attention, so we don't know which driver was at fault

7 A stitch in time saves nine our history professor is fond of telling us.

Guideline 5
Names of stories, songs, chapters, and articles (i.e., parts of a larger work) appear in quotation marks. Names of books, magazines, and movies should be either underlined or printed in italics.

  a. "The Ant and the Grasshopper" also appeared in a collection entitled *Collected Short Stories* by W. Somerset Maugham.

  b. Gail Saunder's "Heart Speaks to Heart Across a Cultural Divide," which was published in the *Christian Science Monitor* in 2000, tells the story of a friendship between two teachers from different cultures.

EXERCISE 20 *Editing for punctuation*
Add quotation marks, underlining, periods, and commas to this paragraph.

   In the essay Whether, How, and Why to Spank, author Dempsey presents his case in favor of physical punishment of children. David Dempsey explains Better to punish children than to be indifferent to them, since it is the neglected child who is more likely to grow up to be a problem. On the other hand, in his book Dr. Spock on Parenting, a respected doctor comes out against physical punishment. If we are ever to turn toward a kinder society and a safer world, Dr. Spock writes, a revulsion against the physical punishment of children would be a good place to start. Whose advice should we follow? parents raising children often ask. The answer to this question is not easy.

APPENDIX B

COMPLETE ESSAY ASSESSMENT CHECKLIST

....

ABOUT THE CHECKLIST

The *Complete Essay Assessment Checklist* that begins on the next page has been provided for you and your teacher to use in assessing essays. Like the checklists in Chapters 3–7, it lists the criteria of a very good essay in three main areas: (1) content and ideas, (2) organization and form, and (3) language. This complete list also describes the characteristics of an average and a weak essay, and provides a point system.*

Assess essays by following these steps:

1. *Content and ideas*

   Read the criteria listed under "Content and ideas" for a very good, an average, and a weak essay. Carefully read the essay you are assessing, and assign a maximum of five points (very good) and a minimum of one point (weak) for the elements in this area, depending on which of the three sets of criteria describe the essay best.

2. *Organization and form*

   Read the criteria listed under "Organization and form" for a very good, an average, and a weak essay. Reread the essay and assign a maximum of five points and a minimum of one point for the elements in this area.

3. *Language*

   Read the criteria listed under "Language" for a very good, an average, and a weak essay. Reread the essay and assign a maximum of five points and a minimum of one point for the elements in this area.

4. *Total score*

   Add up the points you assigned in steps 1, 2, and 3 above. The maximum score is 15; the minimum score is 3.

   Note: If your teacher decides to weight one area of elements, for example, content and ideas, that area can be worth ten points instead of five. If an area is weighted, double the points you assigned to that area.

   *Five points indicates the essay elements for this area are very good; three points indicates a paper with average elements; one point indicates a paper that is weak in the elements being considered. If you decide the elements are better than a 3 but not good enough to be a 5, assign a 4, for example.

COMPLETE ESSAY ASSESSMENT CHECKLIST

A Content and ideas

VERY GOOD (5 POINTS)

- ☐ The writer has thought carefully about the topic and has a clear main idea, or thesis.
- ☐ The writer gives adequate support for the thesis, or main idea.
- ☐ There are no logical fallacies used to support the writer's thesis.
- ☐ The writer's voice is clear because he or she writes in a sincere way and keeps the audience in mind.
- ☐ The reader wants to continue reading to the end. It's interesting.

AVERAGE (3 POINTS)

- ☐ The writer needs to think more about the topic to make his or her thesis and support more convincing.
- ☐ The writer needs to give more support to make the essay clear and meaningful. In addition to generalities, the writer needs to include details that show an understanding of the topic.
- ☐ The writer's voice is not very strong. The writer seems to be writing what sounds good, not what he or she believes and knows.
- ☐ The writer's logic may not be not clear.

WEAK (1 POINT)

- ☐ The writer needs to think more about the topic because it is not clear what point he or she is trying to make.
- ☐ The writer needs to explain and develop points and not repeat the same ideas.
- ☐ The writer's argument is weakened by faulty logic.
- ☐ The writer's voice will be stronger if his or her own beliefs are included.

B Organization and form

VERY GOOD (5 POINTS)

- ☐ The essay has a clear beginning, middle, and end. There are separate introductory, body, and concluding paragraphs. The thesis statement is clearly expressed in the introduction.
- ☐ The essay moves logically in a straight line: The reader can fully understand the thesis and support after one reading.
- ☐ There is balance: The paragraphs all seem to be the right length. No paragraph is either too long or too short for the writer's purpose.

AVERAGE (3 POINTS)

- ☐ The essay has all the right parts but does not have balance. The introduction may be too long, or the conclusion may be too short. The thesis statement may not be clearly expressed in the introduction.
- ☐ The reader has to read parts of the essay twice to understand it because the logic is sometimes hard to follow.
- ☐ The writer needs to make sure that the most important details get more attention than less important details. The writer may need to omit irrelevant information.

WEAK (1 POINT)

- ☐ The essay needs a clear beginning, middle, and end in order to move in one direction. The reader may not be able to identify a thesis statement.
- ☐ The reader needs to read the essay twice and still may not follow the writer's logic.
- ☐ The writer needs to organize the essay so that the main points are separated from each other.

C Language

VERY GOOD (5 POINTS)

- ☐ The writer uses a variety of sentence lengths and types to add interest to the writing.
- ☐ The writer avoids problems of sentence structure including fragments, run-on sentences, and lack of parallel structure.
- ☐ The writer uses English grammar effectively to convey the message. There are few problems of verb tense, subject-verb agreement, word order, count/noncount use, or word forms.
- ☐ The writer chooses vocabulary carefully to communicate clearly.
- ☐ The writer follows rules for spelling, capitalization, and punctuation.
- ☐ The writer uses cohesive devices to make the relationships between the ideas clear.
- ☐ There are no illogical shifts in tense, person, or number. The tone is consistently formal.

AVERAGE (3 POINTS)

- ☐ The writer uses mainly simple and compound sentences.
- ☐ Sentence-structure problems require that some sentences be read twice for a good understanding.
- ☐ Grammar mistakes sometimes interfere with meaning.
- ☐ Some vocabulary is inaccurate, causing the reader to stop and question.
- ☐ Errors in spelling, capitalization, and punctuation slow the reader down.
- ☐ Relationships between ideas are sometimes unclear.
- ☐ There are confusing shifts in tense, person, and/or number.
- ☐ The tone of the writing occasionally shifts to the informal.

WEAK (1 POINT)

- ☐ Sentences are mainly simple ones, and some of them are badly formed. Compound sentences are long and rambling.
- ☐ Sentence structure is poor; the reader must reconstruct the sentences to understand them.
- ☐ Grammar mistakes make the essay difficult to read.
- ☐ Poor choice of vocabulary leaves the reader confused in several places.
- ☐ Errors in spelling, capitalization, and punctuation distract the reader from the writer's message.
- ☐ The writing lacks cohesive devices to tie the ideas together.
- ☐ Illogical changes in tense, person, and/or number make the writing confusing.
- ☐ The writer uses an informal tone that is inappropriate for academic writing.
- ☐ The reader has trouble focusing on meaning and must reread to understand the essay.